LIVING
ON THE EARTH

Eclectic Essays for a Sustainable
and Joyful Future

Bill Duesing

Edited by
Suzanne Duesing

Published in the U.S.A.
by LongRiver Books

I S B N 0 - 9 6 5 9 2 7 7 - 0 - 9 paper

Cover illustration and design by Pamela Meier
Book design and layout by Jean-Marie Dolan

Printed by Thomson-Shore, Inc.

Second Printing, 1997

Solar Farm Education
Suzanne & Bill Duesing
P.O. Box 135
Stevenson, CT 06491

This book is dedicated to our parents
Charlotte, Howard, Marion

and our children
Kira and Daniel.

Acknowledgements

These radio essays are the result of the happy conjunction, 3 years ago, of a space on the airwaves of WSHU (91.1 FM, Public Radio from Sacred Heart University in Fairfield, Connecticut) and a rapidly-deepening relationship with an old friend, who a year later became my wife and partner in life. They would never have come into existence without the support and encouragement of the staff of WSHU, especially Geri Diorio and Tom Kuser, and the opportunity to speak to thousands of people in some of our country's poorest cities and wealthiest suburbs every week.

I couldn't have continued to produce these essays without Suzanne's inspiration, support, and editorial skills. Besides the essential interaction as these pieces were written, she has done a wonderful job in turning radio scripts into readable text. There are lots of advantages to being married to an English teacher.

I greatly appreciate the support Alex Reznikoff and Food for Thought Natural Foods Market, Westport, Connecticut, provided for the airing of these pieces.

We all owe thanks to David Wilk and the mighty staff of LongRiver Books, especially Maureen Owen, Pam Meier, Jean-Marie Dolan, Jay Petersen and Kitty Florey for the fine work they accomplished in getting this book to print.

I thank all the friends, colleagues, authors and teachers who have informed and inspired my thinking. Of course I greatly appreciate the hundreds of letters and requests for reprints I've received. As the media comes under increasingly-concentrated corporate control, it becomes harder to speak frankly about critical issues. Support for public and community radio is increasingly important for our future.

TABLE OF CONTENTS

🍃 Spring 🍃

🍂 Summer 🍃

🍃 Fall 🍃

Introduction

In a complicated society such as ours, it is a rare blessing to run into somebody who is so bold, so perceptive, so powerful in their thinking that it changes your way of thinking forever. Within the pages of this book, you will find the voice of Bill Duesing—a breath of fresh air in a troubled world.

I have known Bill for a long time. We work in the same area and share common goals. I am happy to see that his essays and thoughts are being made available to more people. But this book is not simply a great local book by a local friend. This book should be read by people *all over* the U. S. and the world! It has a powerful force and points to potent possibilities for change on this planet.

In my mind, Bill is the ultimate radical. He never stopped asking "Why?" long after others who came of age in the 60s went on to more "traditional" ways of thinking. His many years of observation, research, and deep thought have given him a perceptive view that we should all take note of for our own health and the health of the planet. What he says cuts through all of the superficial trappings of our society and brings you up short. He connects you to nature, the Earth, ancient wisdom, and human history. It all begins to make sense. This book is not designed to fill you with guilt or helplessness. It is a joyful book, celebrating humanity. It makes you realize that the simple life doesn't have to be spartan, difficult, or unpleasant. Filled with old fashioned pleasures and traditions, it can lead the way to a deeper happiness.

When you visit Bill and Suzanne on their hillside farm, you see these principles in action. Theirs is not a traditional farm with fields of corn, a red barn, a white farmhouse. They grow their own food, raise animals, and make large quantities of the richest compost you've ever seen (with the help of their pigs) using leaves and recycled produce from 2 neighborhood markets in New Haven. Their world is alive, abundant, unpretentious and closely woven into the surrounding landscape. What you may perceive as "weeds" are welcomed and incorporated into the thriving, rich ecosystem. Buildings are handmade and plenty of recycled material is in evidence. The house is small, cozy, warm, sunny. This "simple life" provides a hotbed for complex thought and sincere activism.

This book may make you very angry; it may shock you. Inevitably it will lead you to initiate change in your own life and your community. The changes that Bill talks about are grand, sweeping changes that go deep into the way our society has evolved. All this cannot be done by one person alone... but this voice *can* spark a change of consciousness in all of us. This change has to be initiated on the consumer level. It can't be accomplished by individuals from environmental or organic farming groups standing up on their soapboxes and saying "This is what we should do." It has to come from consumers who demand less packaging and more locally-grown food—from consumers who refuse to buy products that are unhealthy, unsafe, impractical or wasteful. The power lies in all of us.

Bill's clear vision of how humanity can create a safe, healthy and sustainable world for itself is an inspiration. You will want to share this book with everyone you know and send copies to friends. I just kept thinking as I read it, "If everyone understood these problems, things would have to change." It certainly is possible.

Bill Duesing talks about "reality checks." That's what this book really is. Keep it around. The essays are just long enough to get you thinking. It will profoundly influence your life as it has mine.

Nancy DuBrule
October 12, 1993

Owner of Natureworks Horticultural Services, Northford, Connecticut, and Co-author of *A Country Garden for Your Backyard*

Preface

These *Living on the Earth* pieces are a product of my interaction with the beautiful and bountiful hills of western Connecticut and with the vibrant and interesting cities on Long Island Sound that brought me to college in this region over three decades ago.

Since then, both the urban and rural areas have lost much of what made them special and productive. In the cities, many of the neighborhood markets, clothing manufacturers, factories, theaters, truck gardens and local breweries have gone out of business; piles of trash have gotten higher, and poverty has increased.

In the country, sheet metal industrial buildings and ostentatious, boring subdivisions (with their grass monoculture) have replaced small-scale farms, productive homesteads and gorgeous woods. The ever-spreading asphalt of strip malls, parking lots and "improved" roads covers much of the space between the city and the country, providing support for the fast-food and convenience stores, megamarkets and shopping malls which siphon money out of our communities into the pockets of global corporations.

These transnational giants use their profits (recently projected to rise an average of 12.7 percent in 1993 and 10.4 percent more in 1994) to increase their size and control and to further their work of making communities look the same all over the U. S. and, ultimately, all over the Earth. As if this weren't bad enough, we've also discovered that in many cases, the taxes we've sent to Washington, D. C. and to state capitols are used to subsidize the research, agricultural, energy, timber, mineral and other resource costs of the products large corporations produce. Our expenses for waste disposal and recycling as well as for health care and environmental clean-up continue to rise.

People who live in the suburbs (which produce almost nothing and require the use of a car to go anywhere) are in many cases frightened to go into the cities (where beautiful old houses and factory buildings fall to ruin or are torn down). And, despite living with the violence of urban poverty, many city residents are frightened by the creatures, wildness and darkness of the country.

It's terrifying to think of the social, environmental and political implications here and everywhere on Earth, if these trends of the last 3 decades continue for even one more decade.

Yet I never cease to be amazed at the pleasure that even simple things from a bit of nature or a garden, such as flowers, insects, seed pods, fresh tomatoes, fragrant herbs, and farm animals, bring to children and adults everywhere.

One of the clearest lessons demonstrated by our art work as *Pulsa* (7 artists who anonymously and collectively created large-scale environmental pieces in museums and public spaces from 1967 to 1972) was that our surroundings affect our consciousness. Although most of that work involved electronic, computer-controlled lights and sounds, it gradually became evident to us on an abandoned farm nearby that the natural environment (which was retaking the fields), and our organic gardens, provided more favorable effects on consciousness. Since 1972, I have lived on, cared for, observed and learned from a 6-acre hilly farm about a mile from the Housatonic River.

By the time my son Daniel was born in 1975, it became obvious that even on our small organic farm it was not possible to avoid the increasing dangers and effects of modern technology. First there was a plan to transport, over many years, tons of radioactive waste along a narrow, winding and dangerous road near our place. We fought that off, and then there was a proposal for a large regional landfill, less than a mile away. We didn't want these things in our backyard, but we didn't want to chase them into anyone else's either. Our society produces too much that it doesn't want—and too little of what we really need.

These essays are part of my continuing attempt to sculpt a future which increases local self-reliance, ecological diversity, and social justice as well as the beauty of our surroundings and the joy we take in them.

Bill Duesing
October 15, 1993

LIVING
ON THE EARTH

F A L L

S U M M E R

S P R I N G

W I N T E R

The Solstice

December 15, 1990

Next Monday is the Winter Solstice, the shortest day in the Northern Hemisphere and the beginning of the increase in sunlight which will bring us to the Summer Solstice in just 6 months.

On December 21, at 9:43 a.m., the sun will be directly overhead at the Tropic of Capricorn, 23 degrees below the equator in the Southern Hemisphere. The rotation of the Earth around the sun and the relatively fixed orientation of the Earth's axis brings the Tropic of Capricorn closest to the sun on the Winter Solstice. At the time of the Summer Solstice, the Tropic of Cancer (23 degrees north of the equator) is closest, and at the equinoxes, the equator is nearest the sun.

The solstice, meaning the sun halts or stands still, is similar to what happens to a ball thrown into the air. The ball slows down as it reaches its highest point, stops briefly and then begins its downward acceleration. The rate of change in day-length and in the altitude of the sun is very slow around a solstice. These changes pick up speed until the equinox, when the rate of change is the greatest. The rapidly-lengthening days in March are mirrored by the quickly-shortening days of September.

Our distant ancestors were well aware of the time of least light, and of the solstice as the beginning of the road which leads to summer. They celebrated the coming of the light. The Jewish Festival of Lights at this time of year probably evolved from ancient solstice celebrations, and the date of Christmas was placed near the solstice in Roman times to take advantage of the enthusiasm for solstice celebrations. Our seasonal decorations of trees, greens and lights have their roots in ancient festivals which connected people closely with their environment. The reliable, radiant, life-sustaining sun provides a metaphor for many religions.

5

On the Winter Solstice at our latitude (just above 41 degrees north), the sun rises about 60 degrees east of south, climbs to an altitude of 26 degrees at noon, and then sets 60 degrees west of south. This means that the sun spends most of the day shining on the south wall of our buildings. When we put windows on the south side, the sun radiates into our homes.

Practical people will say that it makes sense to have south-facing windows to save energy and cut down on heating and lighting bills. Spiritual people might say we should let the sun into our houses to create a mystical and symbolic connection to the sun as the energy source for life on our planet. Whatever your reason, for the next several months, south-facing windows provide the great sensual pleasure of being in a space filled with the light and warmth of the sun. Given that simple pleasure and the fact that many houses in this area built in colonial times have most of their windows on the south side, it is somewhere between stupid and criminal that we have tied up an enormous quantity of resources in recently built, very expensive houses which have few, if any, windows on the south side.

These houses are expressions of the outdated belief that we can live disconnected from our environment. Regardless of individual religious beliefs, we all need to get back in touch with the Earth in a way more like that of our distant ancestors.

We can now include in our thoughts the image of this beautiful blue and white sphere bathed in sunlight and covered with a fantastic variety of living things working together to make life on Earth possible.

We must share the Earth, home to all the life we know. Only by learning to live in peace with each other and with the environment, can we continue to live on the Earth well into the future.

Happy Solstice.

The Wonder of Life

December 22, 1990

The wonder of it, of the season, is life.
    A birth, any birth, is into life —
the fantastic variety of life that covers our planet
and nowhere else we know —
children and wise women, sheep and hollies,
blue-green algae and maples, rhododendron and catfish,
    It is life —
grandparents and spruce trees —
the bacteria in our mouths and the whales in the oceans —
    It is all life.

Complex, interdependent relationships covering the Earth,
    connecting the nearly invisible with the enormous,
    each living thing providing an environment
    for millions of other living things:
The mycorrhiza on the roots of beech trees and
    the flora in our intestines.

Earthworms, cows, cousins, nematodes,
    oaks and mushrooms,
    each occupying a niche,
    each dependent on others.

An unbroken chain of evolving genetic information
    passed down for a billion years,
    connecting all living things to a common past —
    as surely as all species are connected to all others
    through the atmosphere which is inside every body and
    every green leaf.

We all get our food and get rid of our wastes
    on the same planet.

The cycle of life is birth-growth-death and
    decomposition for recycling —
    making way for more life, releasing stored
    nutrients for the good of life.

This continual cycling takes place
    in the energy flow of the sun.

Dandelions, plankton, wolves, eagles, pines,
    raccoons and honeybees —
        It is all life.

An incredible profusion of living things working together
    to make the Earth habitable.
Just like the bacteria which inhabit the surfaces of our
    bodies and the lichen which decompose rocks,
    life changes and regulates its environment.
The rain forests and the algae on the ocean surface
    regulate the climate.
The air, the soil, water and rocks
    are created or modified by life.
The composition of the atmosphere has co-evolved
    slowly, over a billion years with life on Earth.

In a very tiny fraction of the Earth's history,
    we have used our mechanical prowess
    to change its composition very rapidly.
Our fossil fuel, beef and forest clear-cut habits
    are reversing the evolution of the atmosphere —
    adding methane and carbon dioxide that
    were removed millions of years ago as the
    environment evolved to one where we could live.

With our high-energy lifestyles and our mechanical
    thinking (produce and consume)
    we are rapidly changing the environment
    into one where we won't be able to live.

Carbon dioxide (from our smokestacks and tailpipes)
and methane (given off by colonies of termites in
the tropics, as well as by the colonies that bacteria
have established in the bellies of cows)
are both greenhouse gases.
We know the probable effect of our waste gases
and should be wise enough to make intelligent choices.
Termite mounds participate in the birth-growth-death and
decomposition cycle
in a way that smokestacks and tail pipes do not.

Turkeys, oysters, fine cheeses and wines,
breads and broccoli,
It is all life.

Yeasts, green plants and animals,
nourishing us as we nourish them —
passing down their genetic information
with our culture.

We know the enemies of life:
war, pesticides, high-energy radiation,
clear-cut forestry, asphalt
and lives lived as if disconnected from their environment.

We have the capacity
for the wisdom to make sensible decisions.
We should design a world
which puts priority on important and doable things:
feeding, clothing, housing, educating, healing and loving.

The miracle and wonder of a birth are reflections of
the miracle and wonder of life.
We need to cherish the whole interconnected
web of life on Earth in the same way
we cherish our family and friends
this season.

Hope and the Garden
January 3 & 4, 1992

Having just passed through a time traditionally filled with hope—for longer days, the hope the birth of Jesus brings to Christians, or for sticking with our resolutions—I was rereading a recent *New York Times* article headlined "Hope Emerges as Key to Success in Life."

I started thinking about what for me is the visible sign of hope for much of the winter: vegetable seedlings growing in a south window, and their connection with the year's garden.

Hope has two components: desire and the expectation of fulfilling that desire. We can't realistically hope we'll win the lottery. Although we may want to win, we can't legitimately expect to win because of the long odds. One of the psychologists quoted in the *Times* put it this way: "For us to have hope, we need to have both the will and the way, or the means to accomplish our goal." We all know the way to eat less, spend more time with our children or to fulfill many other New Year's resolutions we may have made, but we have little hope of achieving our goals if we don't have the will, or desire, to do so.

The *Times* article reports that psychologists have found that a high level of hopefulness is a very good indicator of success in college, or of the ability to cope with stressful jobs or debilitating illnesses.

Hope is nebulous, and involves an attitude or a way of thinking. From these studies it seems to be transferable from one area of life to another—from career success to coping with a serious injury, for example. In fact, flexibility is one of the primary attributes of hopeful people: the flexibility to find different ways to achieve their goals, or to change goals if hope for the current one dims. Hopeful people think about setbacks not as failures, but rather as challenges.

It seems likely that one of the ways to build a hopeful way of thinking, which will in turn lead to greater success, is

10

to have had some success in fulfilling a desire, or achieving a goal—sort of like the chicken and the egg. Where do we start to find hope?

Hope seems to be in somewhat short supply these days, except perhaps in the stock market and among political candidates, so let's get back to those seedlings in the south window.

I discovered long ago that one way to make the winter fly by was to start seedlings for vegetables and flowers. Celery, pansies, foxgloves, Spanish onions, early cabbage, and delphiniums all need to be started in February for good production. In March, it's time to start broccoli, eggplant, lettuce, tomatoes, dianthus, dahlias, and some marigolds. Snapdragons, zinnias, salvias, other onions, and petunias also do well if started in February or March.

By the middle of March, it's time to plant peas and early greens outside, and soon after, time to move some of the seedlings to larger containers or the cold frame.

And once April is here, plants are sprouting, blooming and growing so fast that they will absorb all the attention we can give them. After a summer and fall of eating and enjoying the results of February's effort, there are the Thanksgiving, Christmas and New Year's holidays. Then it's January again and time to start ordering seeds and preparing trays of soil for seedlings. However, next year, all this is done with the skill and knowledge from this year's garden, and with the expectation of success based on the previous year's experience.

Although many things can go wrong in the time between the tiny seed and the mature flower or vegetable, there are also many chances, and many paths for success. If you miss the early broccoli, you can always start it in May. If you don't get to plant onion seeds inside in February or March, you can buy onion sets and plant them outside in April or May. The point is that with a little care, almost anyone can have success in turning the contents of small packages of seeds into delicious vegetables and beautiful flowers. Since most of us have a desire for good food or beautiful flowers, this activity has all the ingredients needed for hope—a hope which returns every year and increases with the previous years' successes.

I suspect that this aspect of gardening is high among the reasons gardeners are generally cheery, optimistic and resourceful people. It's also one of the reasons I recommend that you get directly involved with producing food and flowers in your own garden.

The Garden and the GNP
January 5, 1991

R esolved: to garden as much and as wisely as possible and to examine economics in the light of the beautiful fecundity of a garden.

The organic home or community vegetable garden is the most energy- and resource-efficient way to get our food. It also has the fewest negative environmental impacts. With its beauty, productiveness, educational and recreational value, a garden contributes to a more wonderful and livable world.

Almost as important as tending a garden, is to use the wisdom gained to re-examine economics. Economics — the pseudoscience which has been elevated to the level of a state religion today — has become the bottom line in the conduct of human affairs. This imposes limits on our freedom to do what we know is right. Economics has not been handed down by any of the gods recognized by the world's major religions, nor is it scientifically valid, like the laws of physics for example. It is a dysfunctional paradigm for understanding the relationships among human beings.

One of the clearest ways to understand some of the flaws in economics is to consider the Gross National Product or GNP, the total of all the quantified goods and services in the country. It is supposedly the broadest and most pervasive measure of the economy's health. The bigger it is and the faster it rises, so the theory goes, the healthier the economy.

The GNP soars if you drive your car to the store to buy vegetables trucked in from Mexico. It barely budges if you get your vegetables by walking to a garden. The GNP goes up with each beer or cigarette advertisement, and with each medical procedure or ambulance run. The GNP is barely affected if we read or garden with a child, hang clothes on a line or let winter sunlight into a house to warm it. It should not be surprising then that our GNP-driven world is filling with ever more elaborate advertising for such drugs as alcohol and nicotine, and that an increasing number of our children are not getting the parental attention they deserve.

What is measured and rewarded by economics is usually the more capital and resource-expensive, and more polluting course. Continuing to judge and guide our country by a rising GNP is like judging a person's welfare by his or her weight. For the first 15 or 20 years of life a steady weight gain is necessary to produce a full-sized adult. After that, however, weight gain isn't needed, and steady weight gain through adult life produces a very fat person with many health problems.

Like adult weight gain, our rising GNP has produced an economy with an enormous excess of goods and many health problems. Each average American can now throw away a ton of solid waste every year, dump 5 tons of carbon into the atmosphere, and take credit for his or her share of the voluminous streams of sewage, hazardous and radioactive wastes which our economic view of the world has encouraged. The GNP goes up when dangerous wastes are produced and goes up again when they are treated or stored. The more expensive the treatment and storage, the greater the rise in the GNP.

With the GNP as our guidepost, is it any wonder we have problems? The failing banks and insurance companies and the 1980s financial cowboys who rode the fast-buck bronco into bankruptcy are as much symptoms of the failing economic religion as are the homeless in our cities, the disappearing farmers and our troubled, under-funded educational system.

So, although it won't help the GNP much, we all should garden this year. Gardening provides one of our most basic needs, helps our physical condition and our spirits and provides an opportunity to reflect on our individual and collective relationship with plants, soil, water and sunlight.

Because of its structure, the current economic system values waste, inefficiency and complex methods of obtaining basic needs. We must work to evolve a system whose values are aligned with the needs and aspirations of human beings rather than with the values of multinational corporations, government bureaucracies, and greedy moneychangers.

The garden is a great place to start for a productive and peaceful New Year.

Our Wood Stove
January 10 & 11, 1992

This time of year it is especially wonderful to be living in our small home heated by the sun streaming in south windows on sunny days, and an efficient wood stove otherwise.

To keep warm in this climate, we usually need to burn something to supplement the solar energy we can capture in our well-insulated houses. Some folks burn oil from Saudi Arabia or Venezuela; others burn natural gas delivered by pipeline from Oklahoma or Louisiana or use the energy from fissioning uranium in a nuclear power plant. But for 20 years, wood has been my fuel of choice.

The many reasons range from aesthetic and functional, to economic and ecological. A wood fire provides the ever-changing, somewhat hypnotic visual pleasure of television without the commercial brainwashing. Cedar, cherry and black birch logs provide wonderful fragrances as they burn. And the reassuring hisses and pops of a wood fire soothe us to sleep on icy nights.

Now, I don't think we should cut down trees to burn them. But if we care for our trees and forests, we will have enormous quantities of wood which aren't otherwise useful. Prunings from fruit trees, the branches and tops of trees harvested for lumber, dying or crowded trees, and trees cut to let the sun shine into our houses or onto our gardens are all good sources of heat.

When we burn oil and natural gas, we release (as carbon dioxide) carbon which plants took from atmospheric carbon dioxide millions of years ago. When that carbon was removed from the atmosphere, the climate changed. It shouldn't surprise us then, that as we take fossil fuels out of the ground and burn them, we also change the climate. The significant difference is that while it took hundreds of thousands of years to get that carbon into the ground as fossil fuels, we are taking those fuels out and burning them in just a few decades.

When we burn wood, we release carbon which was taken out of the atmosphere within the lifetime of the tree. If that tree is left in the forest to rot, the decomposers—bacteria, fungi and molds—release carbon dioxide (just as a fire does). And when we return the ashes to the soil, we return most of the minerals which the tree removed from the soil. Almost everything else that makes up wood was created by the tree from water and carbon dioxide, in a process which uses the energy of the sun and stores that energy as wood.

To minimize pollution, we should burn only dry, untreated wood, with ample oxygen, in an energy-efficient stove. Many new stoves have a catalytic converter which increases efficiency and cuts pollution.

But back to the pleasures of the wood stove and its many uses. How wonderful it is to experience the warmth of the stove's radiant heat after coming in from a long New Year's Day walk or feeding the chickens. We make our morning toast on the stove's surface, warm up our tea, and keep a large kettle of water hot for washing bodies or dishes. Like the wonderful multi-functional fireplaces in colonial kitchens, our wood stove provides many services, from slow-cooking soups and stews to drying laundry overnight.

In common with many other ancient and simple technologies, wood-burning demands much more skill and knowledge than the dial-a-number thermostat on a gas or oil heater. It also rewards that skill, knowledge and practice with a greater understanding of the important cycles of our planet, and the properties of different woods.

Between my mother's childhood and my son's, our society has substituted for the intimate warmth of the wood stove, an oil fire in the basement or the distant, radioactive fire in the belly of the nuclear power plant. Recently, all 4 nuclear plants in Connecticut were not working, and earlier last year, we had a war to keep oil coming in from the Middle East. Both of these events cost us plenty.

The one-time investment in our wood stove and our exercise in gathering and preparing wood allow us the luxury of always being warm when it's cold outside.

Exports

January 15 & 16, 1993

Exports, Exports, Exports! The Commerce Secretary-Designate told his Senate questioners that he was going to work hard to increase American exports. The current Secretary of Agriculture told the "Agriculture Outlook '93 Conference" that the fortunes of American farmers depend largely upon a healthy international market. The United States already exports the products from 1 out of every 3 cultivated acres.

An editorial in *The Grower*, a publication which serves commercial fruit and vegetable farmers, says, "Clinton indicated he wants to continue to push U.S. food exports, which is the best hope for growth." Last year the government gave $4.5 million to a California winery, over $1 million to a Minneapolis food giant, and lesser amounts to tobacco companies and fast food businesses in the interest of encouraging their exports.

Locally, business groups on Long Island and Connecticut's Department of Agriculture are pushing for increased exports.

We need to ask ourselves if it really makes sense for us to try to solve America's problems by getting the rest of the world to buy more of the products turned out by our farms and factories, or by our financial and service corporations. We already produce more than we can use of many things— which range from wheat, pork and milk, to airplanes, office space and electricity—but this surplus hasn't produced enough jobs to keep us all employed. Sadly, even fewer of us work in challenging, satisfying and really useful occupations.

Of course, this is true, in part, because we have steadily replaced human beings with machines, and heavily subsidized the fossil and nuclear energy and chemical industries. Hundreds of billions of dollars have been invested to create large-scale farms, factories, food and financial networks

17

which turn out a barrage of goods and services. To small farms and businesses in our communities and around the world, this barrage from American corporations seems, in the words of a Mexican businessman, "like a steamroller driving local enterprises to extinction."

To create these excess goods and services, we have been willing to clear-cut our forests, stripmine our hills, abuse our farmland, and put people out of work. And, when our low-cost corn is exported to Mexico under the proposed free trade agreement, Nafta, about a million small farmers there are expected to be driven off the land and into the cities. Cheap, exported food is a weapon which drives local farmers out of business—as surely as cheap, franchised fast food drives out local restaurants in cities and suburbs all over the world.

It seems counterproductive for us to use environmentally-damaging technologies to produce great surpluses of goods and services we can't use in order to earn money, in the hope that *this* will somehow solve our problems.

It also seems dangerous to pin our future on the expectation that people in other countries will have the money and the desire to buy our products instead of their own, or those from the many other nations which are gearing up to compete in the global marketplace.

What audacity to expect consumers in Latin America, Africa and Asia to bail us out when we are one of the wealthiest countries in the world.

And it seems most unlikely that profits made by global corporations in distant corners of the Earth will ever make it back to our schools, health clinics and hungry people.

My experience teaches me that a better way to educate, feed and care for ourselves, as well as to create satisfying work, is to encourage and increase local sufficiency. The garden is a great place to start—a model which is relevant here and everywhere around the world.

Jobs, Work and Chores

January 17 & 18, 1992

"Jobs, jobs, jobs," said George Bush.

"When I was a child, I hated chores, but now I realize that chores are where it's at," said Debra.

Humans need to work to feed, clothe, and house themselves, as well as to care for and educate their children, or other dependents. For tens of thousands of years, we have done just that. It is only in recent history, with the concept of work as a job, that it has been possible to be unemployed. Until this century, most people worked in many ways to provide for their needs. These included: producing food—from gardens, orchards, and maybe a small flock of chickens or a family cow; cooking and preserving food; gathering fuel for heating and cooking; and maintaining shelter. These are chores—the regular or daily light work of a household or farm, the work necessary to sustain life. Many people used to be directly involved in the creation of their own shelter, clothing, furniture, quilts, and toys. Transportation was largely by foot, the food-powered work of walking. Not surprising then that it turns out that walking is the best exercise for men and women who want to take care of themselves.

The western way of thinking that includes capitalism, progress, and technology, has, over the lifetimes of people we know, focused almost all of our work energy on a job. A job is supposed to provide money to buy everything we need. What work energy is left after the job is now mostly used in non-productive rituals such as lawn maintenance, car washing, grocery shopping, taking out the trash, or TV-viewing. To be fair, we should note that today, women, more often than men, are caught in both worlds, holding a job and performing the chores of the household.

In order to fill factory jobs in the first half of this century, our society moved people out of rural areas into the cities. This was done with the pull of good wages and flush toilets in the cities, and the push of industrial agriculture carried out with large machines and chemicals which devalued the work of people on the land. As the factories which pulled people from rural areas close or move to places like Indonesia (to take advantage of workers to whom they pay less than 20¢ an hour) we find millions of people stuck in the city, where many of the traditional skills and activities of humans are useless.

The work that really needs doing includes educating our children (and many adults, too), cleaning up our environment, renovating and insulating decaying and empty older buildings, planting and maintaining trees, and growing food near where people live.

The current shortage of jobs, juxtaposed with so much work that we know needs to be done, shows the skewed nature of our economic system. Not only are the majority of people dependent on some large entity for a job, they are also dependent on large entities for food, shelter, clothing and warmth.

Like the agricultural technologies which devalued the work most people can do, the questionable notion of progress almost continuously makes humans' skills obsolete, as the search for profits drives technological change. More and more jobs take place not in the traditional outdoor natural environment, but indoors, frequently in the context of man-made electromagnetic radiation, toxic substances, and rigid, electronically-monitored production quotas.

Although we share deep concern for people who have lost their jobs, we have to cheer at the closing of factories which make large cars, plastic bags or weapons. We welcome the decline in construction of strip malls, office towers and large single-family houses because we believe the world will be a better place with fewer of these.

We are challenged to find ways to accomplish the work that needs to be done—feeding, clothing, housing, and cleaning up—in a manner which harnesses ancient and traditional human energies and skills to care for ourselves and our loved ones.

George Bush says that we need to create jobs here producing cars or rice for Japan, so we can get money to buy sneakers from Indonesia, fruit from Chile, and oil from Saudi Arabia. Debra (who learned about chores) and her husband Oliver, live in the city in an old house that they are renovating. They have a garden and a chicken in their yard, and a plot in the community garden down the street. Their work as public school teachers is largely focused on empowering students with the abilities to think, write and calculate as well as to grow and cook food, respect cultural traditions, and use their minds and bodies together to creatively solve real problems.

We hope these students will help us create a local sufficiency to replace our current distant-dependence.

Diversity
January 19, 1991

Seeds are living, breathing packages of genetic information. They are the result of fertilization which occurs when the sperm from a pollen grain is delivered to the egg cell (in the ovary at the base of the pistil of a flower).

This union of the male and female reproductive cells (or gametes) produces the seed which contains a new and unique set of genetic information. It is derived from both parents, but is not exactly like either one. This simple process, in conjunction with the selection pressures of the environment, is the substance of evolution.

The male and the female reproductive cells can be from the same flower (as in green beans) or from different sex flowers on the same plant (as in squash) or from flowers on different plants with the male sex cells in the pollen carried on the wind or by insects (as in corn or runner beans).

For about 10,000 years, humans have been active participants in the evolution of plants—especially the plants which are important for food and fiber. Until the last few decades, thousands of varieties of many important plants were cultivated in the world.

The cultivation of wheat began about 7,500 B.C. in the Fertile Crescent of the Middle East which was bombed this week. Seventeen thousand different varieties of wheat have been produced, many of them the result of centuries of cultivation in a specific ecosystem with the best seeds saved each year and planted the next. Plants, weather, agricultural techniques and the human diet evolved together in unique ways at each place on Earth. The variation in plant varieties is related to the variation in culture from one bioregion to another.

In recent decades we have been manipulating the evolution of our food plants at a scale and pace unheard of in the history of civilization. Thousands of scattered varieties are brought together, screened for important traits and bred to produce the hybrid varieties of the Green Revolution and beyond. These "super varieties" are then sent out globally to replace many locally-adapted varieties.

Hybrid seeds are the result of the crossing of unlike parents to bring out desirable traits. For example, breeders may cross a small but flavorful tomato with a large but tasteless variety to produce a large sweet tomato. However, a seed of the hybrid large sweet tomato will more likely produce a plant with small or tasteless tomatoes. Farmers who grow a field of hybrid wheat cannot save their own seed, and are dependent on the seed company for the following year's crop.

As seed companies around the world were swallowed up by large agrochemical and pharmaceutical corporations, hybrid seeds became even more dependent on synthetic fertilizers, pesticides, and machinery for successful growth. The need to become a consumer of farm inputs in order to be a producer of food drove many families off the land and into cities all over the world.

Today, seed companies are going even further. With genetic engineering, one company is producing soybeans that are resistant to an herbicide that is useful against the competing weeds. Selling that seed to a farmer guarantees a customer for the herbicide.

At each step in the advance of seed breeding, the wonderful male/female fertilization processes (which make our world such an interesting and diverse place) are further removed from the farmer and from traditional methods.

These new seeds foster the dependence that multinational corporations are so good at creating. These high-tech seeds, in the hands of the ever more highly capital-dependent, and larger farmers, displace the results of centuries of careful evolution in the relationship between people and the Earth. Seeds of unique varieties are lost. People are pushed into the cities and culture is scattered in the same way fast-food restaurants, television programming and imperialistic nations and corporations have pushed aside time-tested diets and foods, family and village traditions, and more benign ways of organizing society.

Like hybrid seeds, the mass world culture of fast food, fast cars and quick fads produces a dependence on energy, chemical and capital inputs for our basic needs and diminishes the Earth's stock of diversity and traditional wisdom.

Growing and Eating Sprouts
January 24 & 25, 1992

Once we start eating more local food, what are we going to do for fresh greens and vitamins in the winter? More of us are growing and eating sprouted seeds.

When I was a youngster, the only sprouts I knew about were the barely identifiable bean sprouts in canned Chinese food. Now even fast-food salad bars offer alfalfa sprouts, and many people are sprouting other kinds of seeds for tasty nutrition. Sprouted seeds are an alive food rich in vitamins, amino acids, minerals and fresh chlorophyll. Sprouts are an ideal fresh food for the winter. Seeds are easy to store and take up little room. With a few days attention they develop into delicious little vegetables.

Most seeds which are sprouted fall into the two broad categories of legumes and grains. The legumes include (besides alfalfa and the mung beans of Chinese cooking) garbanzo, pinto and adzuki beans, and lentils. The grains most often sprouted include wheat, rye, barley, and buckwheat. Radish and mustard are among the vegetable seeds which are sprouted for extra zest in salads. Start with good quality organic seeds. They are available at a local health food store. Although seeds, and especially alfalfa seeds, may seem expensive, they increase up to 64 times their volume when sprouted.

As their germination demonstrates, seeds are alive, and so they should be treated with respect. Age, high temperatures and moisture can all kill seeds. Sprouting seeds require the same conditions that most living things need—water and air (in appropriate balance), warmth, and waste disposal. Most seeds germinate or sprout underground, so they also appreciate darkness.

To begin sprouting, clean the seeds to remove any foreign matter and rinse them. Soak the seeds for 8 hours in tepid water. A tablespoon of alfalfa seeds, one-quarter cup of mung beans or one-half cup of wheat berries will fill a quart jar when sprouted. A traditional way to sprout seeds is in a wide-mouth canning jar with a piece of screen or nylon mesh over the top, held in place with a rubber or canning band. The seeds need to be moist at all times and must have access to fresh air for respiration. This is accomplished by rinsing the seeds regularly, and letting them drain in the upside down jar. In this way, fresh water and air are brought in and the waste products from the seeds' growth are washed away.

The kitchen counter is usually a good place to keep your sprouts because they need to be rinsed 2 or 3 times a day. Sprouts should be kept in low light for 2 to 4 days (depending on the type of seeds) and exposed to light for a few hours or a day to allow them to turn green, before eating or refrigerating them. Remember that sprouts are alive and will not do well sealed in plastic or stored for a week or more. It is good practice to make only as many at one time as you will use in a few days, and to keep the process going by starting a new batch when you refrigerate the old one.

The most frequent uses of alfalfa sprouts are as a snack by themselves, in salads and on sandwiches. They are also a wonderful ingredient in scrambled eggs and omelets. Sprouted beans make tasty additions to soups, stir-fries, and casseroles. Sprouted grains are delicious in breads, pancakes and oatmeal. Sprouted barley is the raw material for most beers. If we plant barely sprouted grains in shallow trays of soil, we can grow a crop of wheat or rye grass. Cut when 4 to 7 inches tall, it is sweet and delicious and has a reputation for being very nutritious.

In checking with some traditional references, I discovered that a wonderful old standby, *The Joy of Cooking*, claims that producing fresh greens year round in the kitchen is an age-old English custom. The authors give a recipe for sprouted cress and mustard sandwiches. And, what is surely one of the most fascinating books around, Harold McGee's *On Food and Cooking, the Science and Lore of the Kitchen*, gives a more detailed account of the changes that take place as seeds sprout, and their nutritional consequences. Sprouts generally are higher in vitamin C and lower in calories* than the seeds they came from. They have more protein, B vitamins and iron than most vegetables.

There are plenty of reasons to start sprouting today.

Corporate Welfare
January 31 & February 1, 1992

During the winter, even a farmer occasionally has time to read a newspaper. Two weeks ago, *The New Haven Register* carried a story about a new giant mall proposed for downtown New Haven, near the junction of Interstates 91 and 95 and the Quinnipiac River Bridge. According to the story, the mall developers plan to take money out of the pockets of every Connecticut citizen before they even open for business.

In order to build this mall, one of the biggest developers in the country wants the state of Connecticut and its citizens to contribute between $135 million and $175 million in subsidies, or about one-third of the cost of building the mall. That's about $50 from each person in our state. The developer also wants New Haven to acquire land, clear the site, construct roads and garages, and subsidize mall parking and security. Last time I paid attention to mall finances, developers were satisfied with their sweet tax deal which let them

---

* Each food calorie, technically a *kilogram calorie* (Cal.), is the amount of energy (or heat) needed to raise the temperature of one kilogram of water one degree Celsius. One Cal. is equal to 1000 *gram calories* (cal.) or almost 4 (3.968) British thermal units (Btus). One Btu is the amount of energy needed to raise the temperature of one pound of water one degree Fahrenheit.

If our bodies could use the energy in gasoline (with over 100,000 Btus per gallon), 1 to 2 cups would supply all the energy we need for a whole day. Yet many of us couldn't even make it to the nearest supermarket on that much gas. A 40 MPG car would use up that much in about 5 minutes or 3 miles.

pay for the mall over a decade or two, but deduct the cost from their taxes in just 5 years, producing a lucrative net effect. Now they want even more from each of us. No information was given about the impact of additional automotive congestion and pollution that this proposal will generate at an already busy junction.

This winter I've also been reading a very interesting book, *The Resurgent Liberal and Other Unfashionable Prophecies*, by Robert B. Reich, a teacher of political economy at Harvard's John F. Kennedy School of Government. His *Marketplace* commentaries on WSHU led me to his book at the New Haven Library. (The same paper which told of the mall proposal included an article by New Haven's librarian pointing out that during the Great Depression, her library was open almost twice as many hours per week as it is today— but that's another story.)

The mall issue brought into focus a whole range of corporate welfare abuses which it will be to our benefit to understand. As Reich says, "Occasionally, however, the veil is lifted and we are allowed to gaze in wonderment at a private sector whose largest institutions are guaranteed peace, safety, and profits by a public sector ever anxious to please them."

In my own town, for over a decade, the leaders have been spending millions in borrowed money to bring water and sewer lines to once excellent farm land, in an attempt to turn it into a large industrial park. The bills for these benefits to industry are coming due, and money is in short supply. The returns don't cover the bond costs, and town services, particularly education, are being cut.

A friend from Orange told me about his town, which gave a 10-year tax break to Saab, to locate its headquarters there. You guessed it. When the tax benefits expired, Saab moved out of town.

Although the principle remains unchanged, the numbers get bigger as we move to the national level. Reich points out that during the 1970s and into the 1980s, United States taxpayers' foreign aid to Poland, Turkey and Latin America was used not to help the citizens of those countries, but to pay back giant American multinational banks which had made risky loans to these governments. The aid was often used to coerce foreign governments to impose repressive austerity measures on their citizens. It is also likely that the original loans went not to provide basic services to the poor, but rather to provide subsidies to entice foreign corporations into Latin America. It's not so different from the current expensive bailout of the savings and loan institutions.

Reich notes another kind of corporate welfare embodied in the tax code. The more complex and esoteric the code is, the better for very large corporations who can employ skilled accountants to their financial advantage. He tells of the Economic Recovery Tax Act of 1981 which was instrumental in reducing corporate taxes from 26 to 8 percent of federal revenues. The only example he gives is General Electric, which paid no taxes at all between 1981 and 1983, even though it made profits of $6.5 billion. It's no wonder they were able to buy an entire television network. We should also remember that during the 1980s, many of the biggest corporations, while enjoying very low taxes, were at the same time receiving billions of our tax dollars to produce weapons, chemicals and information services to help the federal bureaucracy grow.

Like President Bush's use of a hotel room in Houston as his primary residence to save on his taxes, it's all legal. However, these are the kind of elusive financial arrangements and deals that are guaranteed to impoverish most of us.

Weaving
February 5 & 6, 1993

Here's some good news about education. Last week in Bridgeport, Suzanne and I had a very exciting day in the classroom with her 30 fifth-graders.

These children are as bright, beautiful, handsome, brave, helpful and compassionate as any children in the world. They are also, many of them, very needy—of medical care, love, parents, good nutrition or special educational settings, just to name a few. They bring to school the baggage and debris of our separate, unequal, violent, consumer society. The educational power structure maintains that if we give these kids more and tougher tests, then they'll be world class students, trained to compete with people everywhere for the privilege of supplying our basic needs. Bridgeport is a town where the growth industry is garbage-burning, and the big hope for the future is a casino. More tests? My wife was told that at least half of the state mathematics Mastery Test will be based on the use of calculators. For 3 years she has requested calculators for her classroom, unsuccessfully.

Our friend Diana was the spark for this wonderful day in the fifth grade. She came in to share her skills with the students. She's another one of those farmer/artist people. She and her husband operate a small farm in northern Fairfield county. She raises sheep and turns their wool (whose texture and qualities are the result of years of careful breeding) into clothing and wall hangings with the beautiful colorings of natural dyes.

Since Diana's ambitious goal for the day was to have the students spin and dye wool and learn the basics of weaving, I changed my weekly visit to coincide with hers so we would have 3 adults to work with the students. With thirty 10-to 14-year-old children in one room, chaos is never far away. Sometimes just getting them to settle down can take 15 minutes.

We started by passing out a handful of wool to each pair

of students. Diana explained the washing process and demonstrated how to tease the wool apart, separating it to prepare for spinning. Then each pair got a drop spindle, similar to the kind children in the Andes learn to use at a very young age. Before long, with a little help from the adults, most of the children were successfully spinning the gossamer wool fibers into beautiful yarn. They found ingenious ways to work together, some standing on desks with their partners on the floor in order to spin long strands. In the typical class setting, with one teacher and 30 kids at their desks, it can take a long time to get all the children focused on the lesson. With this hands-on activity, they were all fully engaged right from the beginning. No idle hand or minds here, and few discipline problems.

After lunch, most of the kids took the yarn they'd made off the spindle and wrapped it into skeins, which were washed and then put aside for the twist to set.

We'd made simple looms out of cardboard, and 12-inch rulers became shed sticks. Because the freshly spun yarn wouldn't be dry, Diana had brought various colors of yarn, and with a little guidance, all the children were weaving.

As they busily worked, 2 dye pots bubbled away at the front of the room—one with walnut hulls; the other with onion skins. Before the day was over, plain raw wool had been dyed a brilliant yellow and a deep, rich brown.

It was interesting to see how the different students reacted. Some of the "good students" had trouble figuring it out. Some of the "bad boys" (who can take a full lesson period to get out their paper, or need to be told frequently to stop drumming) were the standouts in terms of their interest and success in spinning and weaving.

Our joy at seeing the students smiling and engaged, working creatively in pairs, was enormous, and matched their joy and satisfaction at learning a new skill and creating beautiful objects. Days later, Suzanne says the class feels more like a family with the weaving theme continuing as they incorporate the yarn they made into their work.

A Shared Vision
February 7 & 8, 1992

As the unusual January fog and rain in central Vermont was blown away by cold, dry winds from the north, 40 community farmers gathered at the Mountain School, summoned by the Working Land Fund to share information and their visions.

Linda, Nan and Jean-Claude came from the Natick Community Farm in Massachusetts, a town educational facility which is a working organic farm producing beef, pork, lamb, eggs, maple syrup, fruits and honey for sale. In the summer, children learn entrepreneurial skills by growing vegetables and selling them at a roadside stand. Each grade in the town's elementary schools has a different theme relationship with the farm, and many community members garden there.

From the Drumlin Farm, in nearby Lincoln, Ward described a 3-year pilot project where inner-city youth grow food in the summer, and Susan told of the 30,000 students who visit that farm each year.

Stephanie and Nancy work at the long-established Green Chimneys School and Farm Center in Brewster, New York. They described their residential program for disturbed or abused children who flourish in the context of a working farm which also serves as a community educational and recreational facility.

Jeffrey and Brian described their work with Land's Sake in Weston, Massachusetts, which provides ecological management for 2,000 acres of community land. Their care of forests not only maintains trails, but also manages the forests for long-term productivity and beauty by ecologically harvesting sawlogs for lumber and firewood. Among their other programs are 2 town farms. On one, middle school students grow food for the needy in the Boston Area. On the other, high school and college students are employed to produce

31

organic vegetables for sale at a farm stand.

Michael directs the "Chili Project" in central Massachusetts which produced the ingredients for and canned 6,000 quarts of vegetarian chili. These were distributed through food banks and soup kitchens along with the 60,000 pounds of fresh vegetables they grew.

At the Southside Community Land Trust, in Providence, Rhode Island, community gardens, a ready-to-serve salad greens business, and a variety of educational and open space projects make productive, beautiful use of abandoned urban areas. The racial and ethnic mix is such that their newsletter is printed in 4 languages.

The town of Narragansett bought a farm for its use, and way up north in Burlington, Vermont, the Intervale Foundation runs a community farm and the Burlington agricultural incubator on fertile soil built with composted leaves.

Kristen is "Farm-to-Family" coordinator for the Hartford Food System. Her program brings fresh vegetables from Connecticut's farms into Hartford's poorer neighborhoods, helping to support Connecticut's farmers as it gets the most nutritional food to those who need it, particularly mothers and children.

Melody from Kingston, New York, Scout from northern Vermont and Suzanne from Central Vermont told of their involvement with Community Supported Agriculture, or CSA. In this system, a group of individuals and families buy shares of a farmer's harvest before the growing season. This ensures an income and market for the farmer, and a reliable source of organic food for the shareholders.

Joe from Foodworks is restructuring an elementary school in northern Vermont with a different historical garden and ecological research station for each grade. I shared our successes in using a farm for education with high school students in New Haven and a garden with fifth-graders in Bridgeport.

Money matters were discussed. Susan (who grows 75 acres of some of the best organic vegetables in New

England) and Suzanne (who grew 3 acres of vegetables for her CSA) both reported making less than $3 an hour for their work, but planned to continue both their farming and educational activities nevertheless.

The message was clear: Farms and gardens are too important to be left to economics. We may be able to get lots of cheap food from far away, but only farms and gardens near everywhere can help manage our community lands, educate our school children, recycle our organic wastes, and bring communities together.

It wasn't surprising that when the visions we had each written on a slip of paper were read, a shared vision emerged: a future where nearly everyone is involved in producing some of his or her own food.

Lessons
February 12 & 13, 1993

Last week I described the joy and excitement 30 fifth-graders and 3 adults found in turning wool first into yarn and then into simple weavings in a Bridgeport class-room. Indeed, the process of hand-spinning with a drop spindle is so interesting and satisfying that I admit to feeling a reluctance to pass the spindle back to a child after helping to get it set up, or demonstrating a certain technique. There is something nearly magical about the way a fluffy, gossamer bunch of wool becomes strong yarn with just a little twisting.

The magic lies in the nature of the wool. Each strand has tiny kinks or curls which grab onto nearby strands and hold on tight as they are spun. Sheep grow their coats of wool to keep warm and dry in the many harsh environments where they thrive. Over the centuries the quality of wool has been shaped by human selection for length, softness or curl, for example. Each sheep's annual haircut produces enough raw material for dozens of socks, gloves, hats, and a few sweaters, too.

We know that wool is a very insulating and water-resistant fiber that for thousands of years has kept human hands, heads, feet and bodies warm. Wool is created by sheep using the solar energy and nutrients collected by—and stored in—the grass they eat. Their waste products—urine and manure—are valuable nutrients on a farm. Indeed, the proper balance and rotation of sheep and pasture can actually improve the fertility of the land while it nourishes the sheep. Ironically, our now frequently ecologically-destructive lawns evolved from sheep pastures on English estates.

In many parts of the world, sheep are also milked to make delicious cheeses. It is an elegant and sustainable system. Whether in New England, the islands of the north Atlantic or Mediterranean countries, the interaction of an appropriate-sized flock of sheep and the land produces landscapes people travel far to see.

We can contrast this traditional and functional way of clothing ourselves for warmth with the alternative of acrylic yarn, made from oil in chemical factories, and then turned into clothing by large machines or very poor people in distant lands.

Back in the classroom we see another lesson and a challenge. Two of the questions these fifth-graders inspire me to ask of any plan for our future are: Will jobs be available for these youngsters when they finish school? Will those jobs be worthy of their talents and spirit?

The head of one of the world's largest chemical companies (based in France) was asked if his country will be successful enough to reverse the trend toward ever higher joblessness. He said that there is an absolute, irreversible shrinkage in the number of jobs as industry has replaced people with large mechanized factories—the way people were replaced with chemicals and machines on farms earlier in this century. He concluded that "there will be no solution to the problem until we change our thinking and our values, until we come up with some completely new ideas about the way our societies are organized." He admits that he doesn't know what the solutions will be, but notes that it is a fundamental challenge for our societies' future.

I doubt that a *good* solution for the future has anything to do with making more chemicals. Although the chemical and fossil-fuel route may turn out an incredible quantity of synthetic-fiber clothing, its relationship with the land, people and environment can't touch the elegance of hand-spun local wool created from the interaction of the sun, grasses, sheep and humans.

That day in the classroom and the pleasure taken by fifth-graders and college-educated adults in a renewable and sustainable way of providing one of our basic needs, suggest an accessible direction for the future—a direction whose elements include solar and human energy and traditional ways of caring for ourselves and for the Earth.

Energy I — *for PACE*
February 16 & 22, 1991

The nuclear and fossil fuel industries are like Saddam Hussein. They invaded our lives and despite repeated warnings of the dangers of their invasion, they refuse to leave.

We know that our fossil fuel habits are causing unhealthy air quality in many of our cities as well as economic pain to the poor and to local governments. The burning of oil, coal and natural gas causes acid precipitation and increases the greenhouse effect, and the spilling of oil despoils our waters. We have nuclear power plants which are almost ready to close and we haven't yet finished the technical and political puzzle that must be solved to deal with radioactive wastes.

The United States includes just 6 percent of the world's people, yet we consume close to 40 percent of the world's energy. Just recently there has been a massive public relations and political push by the giant energy industries for even more control and power over our lives. The oil companies want government subsidies to explore and drill for oil, and they want to produce oil in fragile and beautiful parts of our country. The electric power/nuclear industry wants to build more nuclear plants and burn more coal. These 2 sources of electricity have the greatest long-term environmental costs which our children will bear.

I think future historians may place Saddam Hussein and George Bush on the same side in the war against the Earth. Both of them have promoted the wide use of oil, nuclear materials and chemicals. To the Earth, the dividing line between industrial and weapons-uses is thin. Both leaders are willing to sacrifice their citizens' lives in order to protect their oil interests and save face.

Both leaders have for years taken money away from health care, education, housing, environmental protection and care of the elderly and used that money to buy very expensive weapons of mass destruction. Saddam is willing to spill oil in the Gulf for his advantage. Bush is willing to drill for oil in unique wilderness areas of our Earth to sustain the growth of his oil industry.

Saddam and George have both benefited financially from our addiction to high-energy, oily lifestyles.

An intelligent and perceptive outsider would consider it absurd that, living in one of the most beautiful and productive countries on Earth, we can't keep warm without oil from the Persian Gulf, can't eat without food from Mexico and Chile, rarely go out without oil-derived clothes made in the

Far East, and need to get in a car to do almost everything.

If we install insulation and a passive solar collector on a house, the owner or resident of that house becomes an energy producer, while at the same time the total amount of energy needed and the amount of greenhouse gases emitted are reduced. The owner is also protected from inflation because there is no energy charge for the sun or the energy saved by the use of insulation. In fact, insulation and solar collectors are investments whose return increases as the price of oil increases. Conservation measures mean lower long-term costs to the consumer and less pollution in the environment.

But... the mammoth oil companies, fat with obscenely high profits in the last quarter can't stand the thought of millions of Americans getting off the oil habit, any more than the tobacco industry could stand the thought of people getting off the nicotine habit. Both industries are adept at deploying smoke screens to cloud the negative effects of their products and to minimize the possibility of breaking our addiction.

Let's "Just say no" to more oil and nuclear energy, and use conservation, solar energy and intelligent life-style changes to improve our environment and the quality of our lives.

Product and Process — *for NOFA/CT*
February 23 & March 1, 1991

To understand the importance of organic agriculture, we need to look beyond the difference between the possible pesticide contamination of conventional produce and the possible blemishes of organic produce.

It is a difference between product and process.

Organic farming and gardening work by using the processes that have allowed the Earth to evolve to its current beautiful and exciting state.

Photosynthesis, the growth, death, and decay of an incredible variety of organisms, constant change and the nearly total recycling of materials are the processes of nature and of organic agriculture.

This agriculture uses sunlight, carbon dioxide, water, minerals, local waste products and the genetic information in seeds to build and maintain complex ecosystems. These ecosystems produce food while they build topsoil and fertility, hold water, protect diversity and create beauty and pleasant work.

This contrasts with the focus on the product in our current food system, which in striving for the perfect marketable fruit or vegetable, is willing to use toxic materials and methods such as monoculture, widespread irrigation, and annual agriculture on the dry high plains to produce its product. The results of this approach are soil erosion, depletion of aquifers, pollution of wells, a decline in the diversity and stability of our ecosystems, and one of the most energy-intensive food systems in the world.

Long-distance food shipping, modern packaging, processing, freezing and food-irradiation techniques have put an ever greater amount of energy, time and space between the plant absorbing sunlight and the reversal of that process in our bodies, as energy is released from the food.

Our current food system (and therefore our ability to live) is dependent on Chile's political stability, Mexico's pesticide regulations, California's water resources, Kuwait's oil, a small and shrinking number of farmers, and the very few corporations which control any given commodity.

This focus on product has produced farmers who grow a square mile of wheat and then buy all their food from the supermarket. Peasants in Mexico labor to grow winter vegetables for us on land that used to produce corn and beans for them. Many can barely afford the imported American fast food they now get to eat. The traditional small farms of old and New England, with vegetable gardens, small orchards, chickens, cows and a few pigs, produced most of the fertility for the farm and the food for the farmer's family, with surpluses of several kinds for their neighbors. This agricultural model is nearly forgotten and almost extinct.

Our current system uses fossil fuel-powered factories instead of leguminous plants like peas and clover to obtain nitrogen. We grow lettuce (which is 95 percent water) in the desert and then use oil to move it 3,000 miles to our mouths. We use millions of pounds of chemicals that are toxic to much of the life on our planet, but the apologists for the chemical industry say it's okay because there is little or no residue left on our food. The cheapness of taxpayer-subsidized chemical fertilizers, pushed by industry and their government partners, has caused materials like food wastes, animal manures, and leaves to change from being valuable resources, to being garbage—now a global problem.

The real key to organic gardening and agriculture is a healthy soil, full of living things (6 billion to a teaspoonful) and decaying organic matter. The understanding and care needed for good garden soil is symmetrical with the understanding and care needed by our Earth.

A Landscape Piece
February 28 & 29, 1992

The gentle snow of late February emphasizes our crab apple's arching limbs, the dogwood's gracefully spreading branches, and the ash's stiff uprightness.

Most of the raspberry canes have been pruned, daffodil shoots are poking through the pine needles, and big buds on the Royal azaleas and magnolias promise more beauty to come. *Cornus mas* shows bits of its yellow blossoms, and the swelling buds of the soft maples and weeping willows produce a lovely red and chartreuse haze above the swamp.

In just a few weeks, we'll turn compost and minerals into our garden bed and plant early greens and some peas. Soon, dandelions and other wild greens will be ready to eat.

Now is the time to begin thinking about what you will do with your yard this year.

It may be good to start by taking a walk in the woods. You will see that, left alone, the ecology of our region produces beautiful landscapes.

On your walk, feel the presence of large trees; imagine how wonderful their shade will feel next summer. Come upon a wild azalea, laurel or blueberry in the woods. Look at the always different beauty of exposed rocks wearing lichens and mosses—their patina of age. Enjoy the bright green Christmas ferns against the tan carpet of leaves slowly but continuously composting to enrich the soil. Experience the pleasure of a small clearing with grasses and wildflowers in the center and berry bushes at the edge.

Pay attention to scale and the relationships between plants. Notice also the way sunlight shapes the environment, encouraging dense growth in cleared areas, while pulling the landscape toward a tall forest with a shady floor.

Back in your yard, get oriented: Find out which direction is east, and from there clockwise, south, west and north. Then plan to shade your house from the hot summer sun by planting trees to the east and west and close-in and limbed-up on the south. Evergreens on the northwest side protect against the coldest winter winds.

Create a garden in the sunniest spot to produce food and flowers. Start small, but leave plenty of room for expansion. Once you taste the food you grow, you'll want more of it. Place a compost system convenient to your kitchen and garden for converting their wastes into fertility.

We all need a handy and attractive place to dry clothes in

40

the sun. We also benefit from some screening from our neighbors and the road for privacy. A shaded outdoor table for summer meals, and a covered open space enhance the pleasures of the garden.

Once these areas are outlined, plan paths to connect them, and see what's left. You'll probably want the minimum possible lawn, since there are so many outdoor activities more pleasant than mowing one. Aside from what's necessary for the kids to play on, grass is most useful as a passage and connector. It's nice to have a lawn small enough to be mowed by hand.

Other gardens, trees or shrubs should fill the remaining spaces. If you can't plant right away, sow some oats soon, or buckwheat after the last frost to hold and enrich the soil. Raspberries, blackberries or blueberries are good choices for low-maintenance, multipurpose plants. They have provided delicious fruit for the inhabitants of this region for thousands of years. Other plants can be chosen that are appropriate for the available light and space. Viburnams, junipers and bush honeysuckle invite birds into your yard, and Buddleias, milkweed and Echinacea attract butterflies.

Although the specifics will vary for each yard, the relationship with the sun remains the same. Your garden may be in front or in back. On a small lot, the evergreens might be hollies or rhododendrons, while a larger yard may have white pines or spruces. Be sure to think about the effect trees to your north will have on your neighbor's sunlight.

Wood chips make soft, cheap and mud-free paths which slowly become fertile soil. Stones make beautiful and long lasting walls, benches, terraces and other features. I would avoid plastic as much as possible. It gets uglier all the time and doesn't decompose.

The most pleasant landscapes are those managed with as few powered machines as possible. Hand tools are kinder to our bodies, minds, senses, pocketbooks and neighbors. Avoid chemical fertilizers and toxic substances. The real secret to a healthy and beautiful garden is a healthy soil, full of life.

41

The Pork Report
March 6 & 7, 1992

Pork production rose 8.6 percent in the last quarter of 1991, and 1992 production is projected to rise 4.5 percent above the previous record in 1980. This large supply has caused low prices.

The Pork Report: A Publication for America's Pork Producers is published in Iowa by the National Pork Producers Council. The February 1992 issue gives current production statistics and describes the Pork Council's numerous activities which are designed to increase consumption of American pork around the world.

The article titled "Fat of the Land" in the May 1991 *World Watch*, describes the meat-producing industries in our country. The author says, "Taken as a whole, livestock rearing is the most ecologically-damaging part of American agriculture."

Animals consume 70 percent of the grain produced in the United States. It takes almost 7 pounds of corn and soybeans to produce one pound of pork. The same amount of grain produces almost 1.5 pounds of beef and over 2 pounds of chicken. One pound of lean pork provides about 1,200 calories of energy, but consumes 14,000 calories in its production. The energy used to produce a pound of pork would produce 15 pounds of milk, rice, potatoes, or fresh fruits and vegetables.

It takes over 400 gallons of water to produce a single pound of pork. The water is used not only to irrigate crops, but also to flush away manure. Today's pork comes largely from warehouse-size sheds which hold large numbers of hogs and are built over sewage canals.

The only mention of environmental issues in the *Pork Report* relates to the incredible quantities of manure produced by these large hog operations which sometimes pollute surface and ground water. The Pork Council's Environmetal

Task Force recommends that producers implement nutrient management plans voluntarily, in return for us taxpayers providing liability protection and tax credits.

It takes about 6 months to raise a hog to the market size of 250 pounds. Over 300,000 hogs are slaughtered each day in America.

So, if you ever buy a pound of pork again, picture the energy equivalent of nearly one half gallon of gasoline, and the 430 gallons of water that were needed to produce that pound of flesh.

...Back to *The Pork Report*. These folks aren't just complaining about low prices and too many hogs. They are working hard to increase consumption. In this country, they put ads on prime-time television and in 17 national magazines. They work with McDonald's restaurants on promotion of pork menu items, and provide pork commodity information to school food service programs to increase school pork demand. This is expected to raise the U.S. Department of Agriculture's purchases of pork for school lunches to a record this year.

The pork producers funded a study of fresh pork nutrient values, got the USDA to officially adopt those values and then advertised directly to physicians, dietitians, nurses and other health-care professionals, encouraging them to recommend "today's 31 percent leaner fresh pork."

Not satisfied with just getting Americans to eat more of their product, the Pork Council is working on people in other countries too. After all, total meat production in the U.S. will be 239 pounds per person this year. Beef, broiler and turkey output will all rise, but not as fast as pork production. The Council's president testified in favor of lower subsidies in foreign countries to the General Agreement on Tariffs and Trade (GATT) panel. Since American hog farmers are the lowest cost producers in the world, this will allow them to capture more of the market. However, the hog farmers want to retain the right to impose duties on subsidized Canadian hogs. They also want Europe to drop its non-tariff trade barriers to American pork. These barriers stem from European reservations about the widespread use of antibiotics and other drugs to produce U.S. pork. But if GATT doesn't work out by 1993, the producers aren't too worried because the 1990 Farm Bill then requires that the USDA spend an additional $1 billion for "Export Enhancement."

The difference between the small pig farm E. B. White knew in the 1940s and described in *Charlotte's Web*, and today's hog factory involves years of government subsidies designed to encourage high-energy use, large-scale facilities and chemical-intensive agriculture. Like the airline, automotive, plastic, fast-food, pesticide, office building and weapons industries which have been encouraged by tax benefits and energy subsidies, the pork industry finds itself with the problem of over-production.

It's arrogant of them to think that the solution to their problem is for us to change our behavior—for us to eat more pork.

How Are We Going to Eat?
March 9 & 15, 1991

There is one question which we must answer before we can make any intelligent decision about our future.

How are we going to eat? Human beings who don't have enough food, or enough of the right food, lose energy and become prone to illness or worse. Currently, millions of our brothers and sisters in many countries and climates are hungry.

Ten or twenty years from now, where will our food come from? Many of the economic and political powers in the world think that with the help of GATT and the capital-controlled (so-called) free market, more and more of our food will be produced in what is now tropical rain forest and other Third World environments. Here, with the help of low-paid laborers, chemicals, genetically-engineered seeds, and machinery produced by major corporations, food can be produced wherever minimal environmental regulations and low wages can be found. If everyone's food travels thousands of miles between the agrofactory and a mouth, it gives the oil companies the opportunity to sell even more transportation fuel. Lots of packaging and processing will be required to make the few varieties of agribusiness-grown food into an interesting diet after such a long journey.

Of course, if we are growing our food in the tropics on land that used to produce food for the people there, they either have to grow their food on marginal land or eat food from our country. Agribusiness monocultures don't produce a complete meal.

This system could easily evolve into a future vision where a very few crops, e.g., sugar, soybeans and wheat, are grown on megafarms and processed in giant factories into a wide range of foods fortified with all the vitamins, enzymes and other additives that the wonders of chemistry can produce from oil. In this vision, the entire energy, chemical, transportation, processing, manufacturing and regulatory infrastructure has to be in place and functioning smoothly in order for any of us to eat .

How are we going to eat? For most of human history, except recently, people got their food near their homes by growing, hunting and gathering a wide variety of plants and animals. Fresh, local and seasonal were the characteristics of this energy- and resource-efficient food supply that nearly everyone could walk to.

The giant, multinational, brave-new food system envisioned by agribusiness, commodity traders, genetic engineers and GATT negotiators will be distant, preserved, and the same everywhere for those who can afford to pay for packaging, processing and transportation. Fewer and fewer men

45

manipulating numbers in boardrooms and trading floors will control a system which puts a greater distance between humanity and its essential source of nutrition. And all this will be done in the name of and with the blessing of economics.

If we let the corporate, political and financial elite design our future food system, we will see the continued increase of hunger, illness and environmental damage. We are also likely to see an increase in military actions against native people the world over who are calling for ecologically-sound and equitable use of the world's resources.

It is early March and food is bursting out of the ground in Connecticut. Weeds and delicious perennials provide fresh vitamins and flavor. It is time to plant peas and hardy greens.

How will we eat? We do have a choice. Most of us can participate in producing our food where we live. Or, all of us can participate in, and tolerate, the environmental damage, political unrest, and social injustice of a high energy, distant food system which exploits the people, land, animals, and genetic diversity of our planet in order to produce high profits for a few large corporations.

Cause and Effect
March 12 & 13, 1993

Our country's public sector is in financial trouble. The national debt and the budget deficit keep growing. Government services—from health clinics, libraries, schools and public assistance, to the high-paying jobs our extravagant defense spending created—have been cut and cut again. Increased costs for taxes, health care, environmental cleanup and waste disposal affect nearly everyone.

Yet many large corporations are doing extraordinarily well. A major producer of what it calls "high-volume, low-cost consumer products" boasts that its revenues and net earnings grew at a compounded annual rate of over 23 percent a year between 1985 and 1990. A giant soda and snack-food producer crows that its sales and earnings have doubled every 5 years for 25 years.

Let's consider these disparate statistics as 2 sides of the same coin, and examine the extent to which the private sector profits at the expense of the public sector. Cigarettes are an obvious example. The AMA recently reported that smoking-related health care costs $22 billion a year, including $4.2 billion in direct government expenses. In its annual report, Philip Morris Companies, Inc. boasts that it sells 42 percent of the cigarettes in this country. That means that its profits come with a cost to the public of 42 percent of these health-care expenses. The cigarette maker gets the profits and we get the health-care bill. Of course, our taxes also subsidize the growing of tobacco and the export of cigarettes.

We can see this same pattern, however, in something as seemingly benign as bottled fruit juice. The CEO of a major bottler of single-serve fruit juices (who otherwise had some environmental sense) was proud of his production line which fills 1,800 bottles per minute. In one 8-hour shift, 864,000 bottles can be filled. This amounts to about 140 tons of bottles each day which become trash very soon after they are opened.

Local governments have little choice; they *must* deal with these bottles. I checked with public and private recycling coordinators in Branford and Seymour and found that it costs somewhere between $90 and $115 per ton to recycle glass. That includes collection, transportation, and a tipping fee for sorting and delivery to the end user. Taking $100 as an average cost, every day that this plant fills bottles for 8 hours, in effect, it is sending local governments a bill for over $14,000. If it operates just over 200 days per year, this one production line in one plant adds nearly $3 million to local budgets for trash collection and recycling.

47

When asked about this public cost, the CEO shifted the blame to consumer demand. He didn't mention that his company spends between $10 and $12 million a year on advertising to create that demand.

There has recently been an explosive growth in sales of single-serve, non-carbonated beverages such as juices, teas and waters which are not covered by deposit legislation. (Under Connecticut law, if the beverage company gets the bottle back, the deposit is returned to the customer. If the bottle is put in the trash, however, the bottler keeps the deposit, and we taxpayers pay for disposal or recycling.)

According to the Census Bureau, energy accounts for a greater percentage of manufacturing costs in glass-making than any other industry, which means that it benefits handsomely from the $1,000 to $2,000 per person, per year subsidy we provide to the energy industry. Of course, it also takes a lot of energy to haul all that glass around.

Over and over again the same pattern emerges. Taxpayers subsidize raw materials (e.g. agricultural products and energy) and then wind up being responsible for whatever wastes are produced as well. It shouldn't surprise us that corporations are able to make great profits in this system, as our taxes continue to go up and our services decline.

The March Garden: Peas & Co.
March 14 & 15, 1992

One day it's near 60 degrees and the next the weather report talks of snow. It must be March. The pull of rapidly lengthening days and swelling buds encourages us to begin planting, while below freezing temperatures and snow remind us that winter hasn't left yet.

Nevertheless, it is time to begin gardening. Start by planting seeds of lettuce, broccoli, cabbage, cauliflower, tomatoes and peppers in flats in a greenhouse, in a south-facing window or under lights. A 5-by-7-inch flat of each of these vegetables will provide more than enough plants for most family gardens.

Now is a good time to test the soil. Once you know what you are working with, the needed amendments can be added before planting. Check the compost pile to see if it's ready for use—if most of the ingredients are no longer recognizable and the earthworms have moved in. If it isn't ready, a turning can speed it up. A liberal application of compost each year is about the best way to enrich garden soil.

And it may be time to begin planting outside. One tradition says peas should be planted by Saint Patrick's Day. The seed catalogs say hardy vegetables can be planted as soon as the ground can be worked, meaning when it is neither frozen nor soggy. However, seeds germinate slowly in cold soil, so that planting earlier may not necessarily mean that your seeds will sprout sooner.

Horticulturist and writer Lee Reich suggests in his book *A Northeast Gardener's Year*, that the first planting be done when the daffodils and forsythia bloom. These perennial plants respond to the overall trend in warming and ignore the wild day-to-day fluctuations of the weather. When these yellow messengers of spring put on their show, it's time to plant the earliest crops—peas, turnips, mustard, beets, carrots, chard, spinach, arugula, and dill.

Planted soon, these vegetables become well-established and will grow rapidly in April, about the time you can set out your broccoli, cabbage and lettuce seedlings.

Peas don't produce well in the heat of summer, so they need to be planted early in order to complete their life cycle before then. Besides the old-fashioned peas which are shelled from their pod before eating, two other varieties have become common. Snow peas and snap peas are different edible-podded peas. Snow peas are the thin ones used in

49

Chinese cooking. Their pods get tough as they swell up, but that is not the case with the new class called snap peas. The whole pod stays tender and delicious.

Peas are legumes, which means that they support nitrogen-fixing bacteria (rhizobia) on their roots. This is a wonderful story of symbiosis. Peas provide carbohydrates and a home for the bacteria, which in return provide nitrogen for the plant. The Earth's atmosphere is 80 percent nitrogen gas, but this is not usable by plants. Rhizobia bacteria are able to convert the gas into a form usable by themselves and the peas. Because these bacteria on the roots have to breathe, the air spaces in the soil are very important. Raised-bed gardens are so productive in part because the soil is loosened deeply, and then not walked on again. This is also the reason not to work in soggy soil. Digging in wet soil can ruin its structure, collapsing air spaces that are important to its health.

Most peas like some support to grow on, and some even demand it. They climb by means of their tendrils and do much better with a fence, netting or row of twigs to hold them up. This makes for better air circulation and easier picking. There's nothing much sweeter than fresh-picked peas. Some of the vines have beautiful maroon flowers, although white is more common.

If you haven't done it already, this is also the time to prune raspberry canes, grape vines and apple trees. All of these tend to put on too much growth each year, which if allowed to remain, encourages the production of lots of small fruit very far from the roots. Pruning re-establishes the balance between roots and top growth, and is also important to let light and air into all parts of the plant to help prevent diseases and encourage ripening.

Be on the lookout for those first delicious greens of spring—the wild ones. Dandelion greens are now about 3 inches long, almost big enough to eat, and the stinging nettles (which fortunately lose their sting when cooked) are over an inch high.

The coming of spring is an exciting time in the garden.

F A L L

S U M M E R

S P R I N G

W I N T E R

Spring 1991: Dandelions
March 16, 1991

Journey back to the time when as a young child, you first discovered one of those beautiful balls of fluff which is a dandelion seed head.

In blowing on that seed head, as children have happily done for centuries, you were scattering the genetic information and food reserves needed to produce many more dandelion plants to cheer spring on with their bright yellow flowers.

The dandelion is a very special plant. Its scientific name, *Taraxacum officinale,* means roughly "the official remedy for disorders." It was reported in 300 B.C. that the Egyptians ate it. For over a thousand years in many parts of the world, people have believed that the dandelion has healing properties. Arabian physicians in the tenth century began using it medically, and the Welsh used it medicinally in the thirteenth century. It was cultivated in India as a remedy for liver complaints and for a hundred years, the dried root was an official healing drug in the United States.

Gathered at the appropriate time, the roots, leaves and flowers can all be eaten. The leaves are tasty and tender until the plant flowers. Dandelions are cultivated as a vegetable, especially by the people of the Mediterranean region. The United States Department of Agriculture *Handbook on the Composition of Foods* reports that dandelion greens have more vitamin A per gram than any foods except red-hot chili peppers and liver. They have more potassium than bananas and contain 50 percent more calcium per gram than whole milk.

To honeybees, the dandelion is a very important early source of pollen and nectar. At least 93 other kinds of flying insects visit the flowers to partake of the pollen or the nectar and participate in the fertilization process. Small birds love dandelion seeds; earthworms and other soil life appreciate the extent to which dandelion tap roots open up passageways deep into the soil. English race horse owners and Turkish Gypsies feed dandelion leaves to their animals to build strength and health.

Dandelion stout, which is made from the leaves, is a tonic herbal beer enjoyed by industrial workers in the Midlands of England, and dandelion wine, which is made from the flowers, is reported to be an excellent tonic and extremely good for the blood.

The roots have the greatest medicinal action, exercising a safe and gentle stimulating effect over the whole system, especially the liver, kidneys, and bowels. A coffee-like beverage made from the roasted roots has these beneficial effects without causing wakefulness.

Unfortunately, the chemical companies have viewed the dandelion as an opportunity for profit. The herbicide 2,4-D has been around since World War II. Combined with its chemical relative 2,4,5-T, it forms Agent Orange—a major chemical warfare material used in Vietnam. After that war, the dandelion seemed like a perfect target for a new war. Millions of dollars were spent on full-page color ads, direct mail flyers and television commercials brainwashing us to believe that the dandelion is a horrible weed which it is our duty to kill with 2,4-D, the product of the excess manufacturing capacity from the war. Although there are many reports of negative health effects of 2,4-D, just the fact that it kills or injures most food and landscape plants should argue against its widespread production and use.

This spring let's try to regain our ancestors' knowledge of and relationship to green plants and reject toxic chemical treatment for our planet. The dandelion is the epitome of the beauty, ecological interdependence, nutrition and healing ability of green plants. Viewing the dandelion as an enemy is evidence of our ignorance, arrogance and greed. This spring, let's all appreciate and eat dandelion greens for our health and the health of our planet.

The Vernal Equinox
March 20 & 21, 1992

On March 20, spring arrives as the Earth's orbit around the sun brings its axis perpendicular with a line connecting the centers of the Earth and its energy source, the sun. This positions the sun directly overhead at the equator and means that the sun rises due east and sets due west, everywhere on Earth.

My joy at the coming of spring (and its demonstration of the sun's power to warm our Earth and cause plants to burst forth with flowers, fruits and leaves) is tempered by the energy news from America. It becomes clearer all the time that a great disparity exists between the interests of the average citizen in our region, and the interests of the fossil and nuclear energy industries and their representatives in government.

It has been reported that Saudi Arabia and its American oil company accomplices are pumping enormous quantities of cheap oil with the short-term goal of getting their friend George Bush re-elected, and the long-term goal of discouraging us from investing in sensible, long-overdue energy conservation measures. Using less energy would simultaneously save us money, improve the quality of our lives, reduce pollution, and increase our independence from Middle Eastern politics.

A barrel of oil, which contains 42 gallons, currently costs less than $20.

Last April, *Scientific American* published an article titled "The Real Cost of Energy." It pointed out that even during the peaceful year of 1989, the Department of Defense spent between $15 billion and $54 billion of our tax money to safeguard oil supplies in the Persian Gulf. The Gulf War greatly increased the expenditures last year. Even the lowest of these estimates adds over $23 to the price of each barrel of imported oil. If we paid directly for that, the price of gas would more than double, and we would be motivated to change our habits (and our cars) to save money. But the great free marketeers in the White House wouldn't let that happen. Instead, the marketplace is short-circuited. At least 55 percent of the real cost of oil is paid for with our taxes and with diminished services, over-crowded classrooms and closed public libraries.

If other hidden costs such as tax credits, environmental degradation, health-care expenses and lost employment are taken into account, each person in America pays between $400 and $1,200 per year to subsidize the fossil fuel and nuclear industries. This is in addition to what we pay directly for oil, gas and electricity.

The Energy Bill which was just passed by the U. S. Senate, while modestly encouraging conservation and renewable energy, says that it is acceptable to import 50 percent of our oil, and calls for development and commercialization of an advanced nuclear reactor and one-step licensing for nuclear power plants. It also sets up the United States Enrichment Corporation, a wholly-owned subsidiary of the government, for the purpose of enriching uranium and marketing it to "qualified" domestic and foreign persons. Other government agencies are instructed to promote uranium exports actively and quickly.

We know that uranium creates dangerous conditions for human beings. Surely it is not in the interest of the vast majority of the Earth's inhabitants to have our government spreading the stuff around. It is, however, in the interest of the large corporations which manage and mismanage government atomic programs. Many of them have been convicted of fraud or bribery, been responsible for large scale environmental disasters, or both.

After 40 years, neither Connecticut (nor the United States) has yet been able to solve their radioactive waste problems.

Fortunately, there is a possible solution. The cheapest way to meet the demand for electricity is with conservation. It costs less to free up a kilowatt hour of electricity with conservation than it does to obtain it from imported hydropower, completing a partially-built nuclear power plant or building a coal-fired plant. You can observe the power of conservation for yourself. Next time one of your incandescent bulbs burns out, replace it with a compact fluorescent one, which uses one third to one fourth of the energy to produce the same light and lasts 10 times as long as the incandescent bulb. Over its 5-year life, each efficient bulb will pay for itself and save you about $50 more while it prevents the burning of nearly a barrel of oil.

We know that we can dry our clothes without producing radioactive wastes or greenhouse gases by using an inexpensive clothes line. We can keep our homes comfortable in the summer by planting trees, which also avoids the use of ozone-destroying chlorofluorocarbons (CFCs). One-story shopping centers could use natural light for illumination—and on and on with solutions which simultaneously improve the quality of our lives and our environment and put the power back in our hands.

The Mint Family
March 27 & 28, 1992

One of the surest ways to begin a lifelong relationship with plants is to grow a few herbs. Although an herb, technically, is any plant that dies down at the end of the growing season without producing persistent woody stems, I use it here to mean a plant valued for its medicinal, savory or aromatic qualities.

These plants, which have been our intimate companions on Earth for thousands of years, entice us with their aromas and flavors, their delicate beauties, and the complex web of uses, reputations and symbolisms which have evolved around them.

The mint family is a good place to start your love affair with herbs. Basil, marjoram, oregano, bee and lemon balms, rosemary, lavender, sage, thyme and of course the mints are among its flavorful members.

Although all of these mint family plants have in common a square stem, opposite leaves, flowers with a protruding lower lip, and all produce essential oils in hairlike glands on the surfaces of leaves and stems, they have a variety of growing habits. Basil (one of the easiest to grow and a good herb to start with) is a tender annual which likes a lot of sun and grows up to 2-feet tall. We usually start a few plants inside, but the main crop is sown directly in the soil after the last frost. You can start to pick it in about 6 weeks, and if you keep pinching off the growing tips to use in cooking and salads, a basil plant will grow bushy and produce until fall's first frost. Because it is so good in a fresh tomato salad, we plant some basil in with the tomatoes. Dried basil from the garden brings the wonderful taste of summer to winter cooking, as does pesto, which we make and freeze in late summer when this herb is most prolific.

The true mints, which give this family its name, are perennials which spread by underground or surface runners and can take over a garden if not contained. They will grow in full sun or along shady streams. Vigorous peppermint can reach to over 2 feet high, while Corsican mint barely grows higher than an inch. Spearmint was probably the earliest mint to be used medicinally; its use in soothing the stomach was well-established 3,500 years ago when the *Ebers Papyrus*, the world's oldest surviving medical text, was written in Egypt. In Biblical times, mint was accepted as payment for taxes, and from Palestine, mint spread into Greece (where it became entwined with Greek mythology) and eventually into Roman lands and the rest of Europe.

Similar medicinal uses of mint were discovered by the ancient healing traditions of China, India, and North America, as well as Egypt. Menthol, from peppermint oil, is an ingredient in common brand-name digestive aids, pain-relieving skin creams, and decongestants.

Other mints include apple, horse, mountain, orange and cat. The latter is also known as catnip. It is easy to make an herbal tea by pouring boiling water over a variety of fresh picked mints. When it cools, it is strained into jars and refrigerated. It is a refreshing, healthful and inexpensive summer drink for adults and children.

Frequently I add leaves and flowers from two kinds of balm plants to this tea. Bee balm or *Monarda didyma* is a North American native of the mint family which can grow as tall as 4 feet. Its red, lavender or pink flowers are so showy that it is frequently planted in flower borders. Hummingbirds often visit the clump by our door. The other balm is lemon, a vigorous, bushy perennial plant with a very lemony fragrance. While not as showy as *Monarda*, it is a flavorful addition to herb teas.

Lavender, sage, rosemary, thyme, and the savorys—winter and summer—have been used since classical times for their fragrances, flavors and medicinal properties. All except for summer savory are woody perennials which are a bit harder to grow. They are native to the Mediterranean region and do well with plenty of sun and a well-drained, limed soil. Of these herbs, only rosemary isn't hardy here. It must be taken inside to survive the winter.

Motherwort, pennyroyal, hyssop, and horehound are also members of this remarkable plant family.

Members of the mint family and many other herbs have been found to be useful in healing, tasty in the diet, and fragrant in the environment by humans all over the world for thousands of years. While some scientists find evidence of the effectiveness of many herbal medicines, our narrow-minded public servants in the Food and Drug Administration have banned some effective herbal ingredients and are stifling the discussion of medicinal uses and possible side effects of herbs.

At least so far, they can't prevent us from growing and using them based on the wealth of information available from traditional cultures.

Lettuce
March 30, 1991

L ollo Rosso, Curly Oakleaf, Red Sails, Buttercrunch, Red Riding Hood, Salad Bowl, Sangria and Rosalita are just a few of the lettuce varieties available to the home gardener.

One catalog from a New England seed company lists over 50 different varieties of lettuce, including ones especially suitable for spring, summer, and fall planting as well as other varieties for cutting and for greenhouse production. These varieties fall into 4 general types: looseleaf, butterhead, crisphead, and romaine. Depending on the type, they produce a crop in between 6 and 10 weeks, but they all can be eaten sooner as you thin the small plants or harvest the outer leaves for a salad.

Lettuce prefers cool weather; the heat and dryness of summer cause it the most stress. Lettuce can be planted outside now, or started inside or in a cold frame for transplanting outside in about 3 weeks. Plant this weekend, and you'll be eating thinnings by the end of April and harvesting mature lettuce by the end of May. If you plant some seeds every 2 to 3 weeks, you will have a continuous supply of lettuce until October.

Lettuce is a very beautiful plant, especially the red-leafed varieties. Consider planting a few seedlings in sunny spots among your foundation plantings or in your perennial garden. A little shade, especially in the middle of the day, helps lettuce in the summer.

A loose, fertile soil with plenty of compost and a near neutral pH will grow delicious lettuce. The warmer the weather, the more important the moisture-holding capacity of the soil becomes.

Although so many varieties of lettuce can be grown here easily for 6 to 8 months a year, and greenhouses produce lettuce commercially year-round, most of the lettuce eaten in Connecticut is the iceberg variety grown in the deserts of California and Arizona on huge corporate farms. Iceberg lettuce is over 95 percent water (the highest percentage of any lettuce variety) and is the lowest in vitamin and mineral content. Why then is this lettuce grown in the desert and, using up non-renewable fossil fuel, transported 3,000 miles to our region where we can easily grow more nutritious and beautiful lettuce and where water is a plentiful resource?

One explanation is that our tax dollars built and paid for canals and aqueducts to bring water to the giant farms, built and paid for cross-country highways and subsidized oil production. Iceberg lettuce is the variety most tolerant of long distance trucking, and we have tolerated the pollution caused by chemical growing methods and the 3,000 mile truck journey, which contribute to the greenhouse effect, acid rain and urban smog. These large farms require a low-paid, menial labor force.

As we look forward to a vision of our grandchildren's world, it makes more sense to grow lettuce locally than to truck it from the desert. Local lettuce is fresher, more nutritious, saves energy, minimizes pollution and creates meaningful work close to home. Lettuce production in the desert means higher taxes, more energy-use, more pollution, and lower quality food.

Plant some lettuce soon. Buttercrunch and Red Salad Bowl are delicious varieties which are easy to grow. If you can't plant lettuce this spring, find gardeners or farmers who can and support local food production by buying their produce.

Investment
April 3 & 4, 1992

What shall we do with our money? When we have more than we need, a common practice is to invest it somewhere so that it will be safe and grow in quantity for some later purpose—our child's education or our retirement, for example.

In the past, we could put our money in a local bank to collect interest. The bank or savings and loan company would then lend this money to families or businesses in our community. Today, if it hasn't gone belly-up, the local bank is likely to be owned by a large, distant holding company with no ties to the community. In the 1980s, our money was increasingly used by banks for highly speculative construction projects such as energy-intensive, see-through office buildings and expensive housing or to buy junk bonds to assist in a wave of leveraged buyouts.

We know what happened. Not only is much of our nation troubled with empty office buildings and strip malls (each with an asphalt parking lot), but billions of dollars of tax money have been spent to bail out these financial institutions and to transfer their assets, at bargain basement prices, to other institutions. Leveraged buyouts resulted in reduced profitability, safety and/or quality in such diverse places as supermarkets, petrochemical plants, and local newspapers.

With the decline in interest rates, and the current disgust with the S&Ls and banks, more people are investing in the stock market, buying bonds, or collections of stocks and bonds known as mutual funds.

The major financial weeklies advise us to invest our money in stocks like the Philip Morris Companies, Inc., a tobacco and food giant whose impressive and steady growth make it a good bet. In 1990, this company produced enough cigarettes to provide over 100 of them for each of the world's more than 5 billion people. Its food division produced enough products to provide 3 pounds of processed, shipped-in food in a variety of plastic packages for everybody on Earth, which all 5.3 billion of us could wash down with 3 cans of beer, our share of the equivalent of over 2 billion 6-packs made by its brewing division in one year. Pretty impressive.

We may want to spread our investment around by putting our money into a mutual fund. Once we choose a fund, the particular investments are out of our hands, as they are with most workplace retirement plans. The fund's professional managers will transfer the money to firms which best meet their goals. These investments frequently include tobacco and food giants and companies which produce some mix of drugs, health-care products, pharmaceuticals, and agricultural chem-icals. The more chances a company has to develop a stable of drugs which are taken daily by a large number of people for the rest of their lives, the greater the potential for profits— *and* the potential for higher health-care costs. Other hot investments by funds these days are fast-and junk-food com-panies and retailers who bring the results of low-paid south-east Asian labor to upscale malls. (Think of the irony of this scenario: We see many of the children of our cities, faced with poor or non-supportive homes and ineffective schools, spend-ing $100 for a pair of sneakers which were made by a person earning less than 20¢ an hour. The potential for large profits for the corporation in the middle comes in the context of misery at both ends.) Oil, gas and telephone stocks are also recommended now. Weapons-makers used to be.

The discordance between recommended investments and the general welfare of society is disturbing. As individuals and institutions attempt to maximize their gain by investing, it seems that more and more often, that gain comes at the expense of the larger community.

Take the Philip Morris Companies as an example. By investing in this company, we are betting on its success: on an increase in the sale of cigarettes, processed food and beer. It's been a good bet for years. It's also a good bet that this success will increase health-care costs, the energy and packaging expenses for our food, and waste-disposal costs. (Just the non-biodegradable filters from one year's production of Philip Morris' cigarettes, placed end to end, would reach around the Earth at the equator over 350 times. That's a new 8-foot wide band of used filters around the globe every year.)

How should we invest our money? Socially responsible mutual funds offer one solution. What will probably be more successful in the long term is to make less money, and invest our time and energy directly—in our families, in creating fertile, diverse and productive gardens, farms and ecosystems in our communities, and in directly addressing our society's problems by volunteering in schools, reading to children, and experiencing the positive health effects of changes in our life-styles and eating habits.

The Reasons to Garden
April 10 & 11, 1992

It feels good to get our hands into the soil again. Late snows and freezing temperatures kept us out of the garden longer than usual this year. Last weekend though, we found the soil in wonderful condition (warm and with just the right amount of moisture) as we planted early greens and peas.

We also found some treasures left from last year's garden. A row of turnips we'd been using for greens into December has lovely rosettes of tasty leaves. We found garlic we'd missed at the harvest. We lifted it, took some inside to cook with, and separated and replanted the rest. We also discovered parsnips, just starting to put on their second year's growth to flower and reproduce. Sautéed in butter, they were delicious.

Recently, I asked the 28 students in Suzanne's fifth-grade class at Hallen School in Bridgeport to list some reasons to grow a garden. Over the course of the school year the students have harvested produce from the garden started by last year's class. They've also planted flower and garlic bulbs with the second-graders, sown a winter cover crop of rye, made compost and studied its processes, and grown rye inside in different media, i.e., compost, soil, sand and clay. Currently they are excited by growing seedlings of many garden vegetables and flowers for spring planting. We hadn't discussed the benefits of a garden, except perhaps to talk about saving money and transportation energy by growing lettuce in Connecticut instead of in California's deserts.

I was astounded and moved, by the reasons they provided and the quickness with which they produced a long list. These children want to garden:

> to eat
> for beauty
> to save money (instead of going to the store)
> for health
> to provide a use for food wastes, that is, compost
> to see something new
> to have fun
> to earn money
> to feed others
> to become more responsible
> for experience

65

to learn
to feel good about themselves
to produce more seeds
to do something good for the environment —
    you don't have to drive and can avoid packaging
    if your food is near your home
to keep busy
to save energy
to impress family and friends
because fresh vegetables taste better
to win contests at fairs
because the food is fresher and more nutritious.

These fifth graders understand the reasons to garden. And, judging by the enthusiasm with which they show me their seedlings, growing plants generates excitement.

Two days after this lesson, I was visiting a client in New Haven who is a successful lawyer, still practicing well past normal retirement age. As soon as he greeted me, he took me down into his basement. There, just beyond clothes drying on a rack in the boiler room, were his seedlings, hundreds of them, growing under lights — vegetables, herbs, and flowers — most for his own garden, but some for his friends, too.

The near miracle of the growth of seeds, with their promise of beauty, nutrition and pleasant activity for the rest of the year, brings the same excitement to this well-to-do 70-year-old as it does to fifth-graders from Bridgeport. This excitement has been shared by gardeners throughout history, all over the Earth.

Since tax time is near, it may be useful to point out that, like the heat the sun delivers to our south windows in winter and the air conditioning that trees provide in the summer, food from our gardens is really tax-free income. When we do for ourselves and for our families, we receive full value for our labor; we avoid the costs of subsidies and regulations which have become such a large part of everything else we do.

Doing more for ourselves and our community is consistent with what, more and more each day, seems like our only hope: to withdraw money and power as smoothly and quickly as possible from Washington and Wall Street, to shrink the political and financial bureaucracies which have ballooned to fill the space between us and the real world.

Get your hands into the soil this weekend. Plant some seeds for your health, pleasure and sanity.

Mid-April Garden Update
April 12 & 13, 1991

It is mid-April and things are growing quickly in the garden.

For the last month, most of the action has been underground. Now, as the warmth of spring moves into the ground, bulbs and perennial roots send up shoots and flowers and seeds begin to sprout.

The peas we planted on St. Patrick's Day are up about 2 inches. Spinach, carrots, dill, lettuce, turnips, and arugula planted in the past two weeks have developed their seed leaves, and the shallots are poking through. Garlic planted last October is now 8 inches high, and the perennial members of the onion family—chives and multiplier onions—have been available to add zest to our cooking for weeks now.

Dandelion greens and stinging nettle tops are near the peak of their nutrition and flavor. Sorrel leaves are ready for a refreshing snack right in the garden, or as the primary ingredient in a delicious French soup. Rhubarb plants unfold large leaves on beautiful red stems. Turnips and kale left from last year provide tasty leaves on their way to seed production. We will plant potatoes and more hardy greens in the next few weeks, and will set out broccoli, cabbage and cauliflower plants soon.

The raspberries have been cut back to about 3 feet to encourage good fruit production, and the grapes have been pruned to 4 branches each.

This time of year (when plants are so full of life, and the moisture levels are high) is a good time to plant or transplant perennial flowers, shrubs and trees.

At the Hallen School in Bridgeport, 1,000 square feet of asphalt were removed and soil and manure brought in to create a garden. With help from the second-graders, the fifth-graders turned in the manure with shovels and created beds and paths. They planted several kinds of lettuce, onions, peas, radishes, two kinds of raspberries, a lilac, day lilies and irises. Sunflowers, tomatoes, broccoli and collards will soon follow. The garden engages and excites the students' minds and bodies in a way that is impossible in the classroom. Science and math lessons are everywhere. Even if we didn't need food to eat, or need to learn how to care for and nurture the Earth, the garden would be a successful educational tool. A garden should be part of every school's learning environment.

Keeping a record book is one of the most useful habits the beginning gardener can practice. The number of variables in the garden is enormous. Each kind of vegetable has several, or many varieties. There are numerous places to buy seeds and a wide range of planting times. Soil fertility, drainage and sunlight can vary in different beds or parts of the garden. Cultural practices and growing methods vary also, and the weather is different each year.

Without records, you may not remember which type of tomato tasted so good and was so prolific, or which carrot didn't have much flavor. You may find that your onions didn't get very big, and discover in your records that you planted them at the end of May, which is too late. You could find that the peas you planted in March didn't produce any earlier than the ones planted in April. My records indicate that the flowers are about a week ahead of last year now. Is it the milder winter, the very warm weather this week, or a change in the climate?

Engage your mind and body this year in a nourishing and productive activity: garden where you live, or work, or at a school. In stressful times, the garden is a haven.

Earth-Day Economics
April 16 & 17, 1993

Next week, people around the world will celebrate Earth Day. Although a host of environmental problems face our planet, most fall into two categories: the destruction through consumption or development of desirable resources (e.g. forests, intact ecosystems, the ozone layer and biological diversity) and the creation of undesirable products (e.g. greenhouse gases, solid wastes, and air, soil and water pollution).

These problems are predictable if we understand the shortcomings of the discipline of economics itself. Using economics to guide the development of our society is like using the rules for football to guide the birth of a baby—a dumb idea which is likely to turn out badly. Economics is very good at measuring what it can measure, but most of the really important things are outside its ken. And therein lies the problem.

Economics readily admits that negative and positive externalities are not included in many transactions. Negative externalities (the costs of a transaction which aren't paid for by its participants) include such things as government subsidies, pollution and ecosystem-destruction. When we buy electricity, for example, we don't pay for the full cost of the energy and tax subsidies used in its production, or for the greenhouse gases or radioactive wastes generated by the power plant. These costs are borne by our taxes and the environment. They are not included in our electric bill. By ignoring negative externalities, economics not only encourages a shift of costs to government and the environment (in order to make each transaction more profitable), but also fosters overproduction—further burdening the public sector.

And, most economic transactions fail to take into account positive externalities, such as the value of forests in protecting diversity, producing oxygen and moderating climate. These benefits come free-of-charge with the forest, but are destroyed if the forest is cut. Because the value of the forest's benefits isn't included on the timber company's balance sheet, economics encourages destruction of the public good for private gain.

By omitting negative and positive externalities from most transactions, economics has the unfortunate tendency to shift costs from the individual to the many, and to shift benefits from the many to the individual. This has been, and continues to be, devastating social policy.

For example, we can cool our buildings with either well-placed trees or with air conditioners. When we plant trees to cool our houses, positive externalities result (i.e. oxygen, cleaner air, habitat for wildlife, and soil and water protection). When we buy electric air conditioners, negative externalities result (like noise, greenhouse gases or radioactive wastes from electricity production and ozone depletion from CFCs).

If we look outside the monetary transaction of cooling our houses, planting or allowing trees to grow is obviously better because it increases beneficial services and minimizes pollution. Public benefits increase while public costs decrease.

Since economics ignores these externalities however, and focuses on the dollar value of the transaction itself, it encourages the purchase and use of electric air conditioners because they have more economic value. Economics strives toward bigger numbers.

One of Earth Day's important lessons is to pay attention to the externalities and break away from economics' narrow view. We should ask where something comes from and what happens when we're done with it. We should be aware of the whole life cycle of the goods and services we consume.

Celebrate Earth Day this year on your town green, in your school or community and in your own home.

The Direction of Nature
April 17 & 18, 1992

As we consider our environment on Earth Day, we need to determine what is important and how we will judge our success.

The constant in our environment is change. Is that change toward greater fertility and diversity nearly everywhere, or is it in the opposite direction?

Just north of our farm lies an abandoned hayfield. It hasn't been farmed in the true sense for the 20 years I've lived next door. It was cut annually for hay until some time in the last decade, but nothing was returned to the field to compensate for the removal of the hay, and the minerals and organic matter it contained. With this removal, the soil became less fertile and more acid. The hay became less nutritious, and had more unpalatable weeds. Eventually, the haying stopped.

Now that this field isn't cut, it is filling in with a variety of vegetation. Eastern redcedar trees and autumn-olive shrubs are the largest and most prominent plants, with spacing and patterns a fractal ecologist will understand. These are pioneer species, sturdy and sun-loving. The berries they produce attract mammals (whose paths crisscross the field) and birds, including an occasional pheasant. The wildlife leaves its manure, which boosts the fertility of the soil. Blueberries, dewberries, multiflora roses and cherries grew from seeds in bird and mammal droppings.

These new plants provide shade from the summer sun and shelter from the winter winds, pleasant features that weren't there before. As these pioneer species moderate the climate of the field, seeds contributed by hickory, oak, crabapple, ash and dogwood trees along the stone walls will begin their growth into a forest, and eventually shade out the cedars and autumn-olives. All the while, the fertility of the soil is being built up as a growing population and diversity of soil organisms decompose leaves, needles and manure.

Harvest without return was destroying this field. Left alone, nature is healing it, moving it steadily in the direction of greater fertility, and an ability to capture and store more of the sun's energy. Along the way it provides food and good homes for ever more living things. We could speed up the healing with the addition of minerals, manures, seeds or plants.

Although a well-managed hayfield which includes legumes and has had minerals and nutrients replaced can remain productive for years, that poorly cared-for hayfield might be viewed as a severe injury to the native forest of Connecticut. It is healed—that is, returned to forest—by the diversity of life in the area, in dynamic response to sunlight, rainfall and temperature conditions.

If a tree or shrub is removed, its space will be quickly taken. Like the field's recovery, or the recovery of the forests of New England after the last ice age, given the climate of our region and its genetic resources, a forest will be restored. The time it takes depends on the size of the wound and other complicating factors. Areas which are very large, are paved or have been doused with chemicals may take much longer, but they too will heal. They will return to forest.

Which brings us to another important notion. It is not so much that the Earth is in trouble—that we need to save the Earth. It, after all, evolved from a lifeless, rocky sphere, and has recovered from asteroid impacts and glaciations without our help. Our ability to live here and the natural systems which sustain us, are at risk. A vast majority of all the plant and animal species that have ever lived on Earth are now extinct.

In light of the rapidly growing population of the Earth, we need to firmly set our sights on an environment which can grow in diversity and fertility, and will be able to continue to provide food and shelter for a variety of beings, including ourselves.

As Wendell Berry says at the end of his book, *The Unsettling of America*, "For our healing we have on our side one great force: the power of Creation, with good care, with kindly use, to heal itself."

Earth Day: Membranes
April 19 & 20, 1991

The outer shell of your house or apartment can be thought of as a membrane.

Membranes are technically the thin layers of phospholipids and special proteins which surround each cell in a living organism. Their role is to keep the contents of the cell separate from the rest of the organism, while permitting the orderly exchange of food, wastes, information and essential gases.

The doors of your house allow the controlled flow of

people and groceries in, for example, and wastes out. Phone and cable wires are special channels which admit information, and pipes and wires bring in energy. Windows let light in, but keep warmed air from flowing out. That is in part because glass is transparent to a broad spectrum of visible light, but is opaque to the lower energy of the infrared reflected energy. This simple phenomenon is called the "greenhouse effect," and is the reason why houses can be heated by the sun.

Thinking about your house as a membrane may help you to understand more about what physician and author Lewis Thomas calls "The World's Biggest Membrane." The Earth's atmosphere is not only the biggest membrane, it is also the most important one. Without the atmosphere there could be little life on Earth. Without life, our atmosphere would be radically different. After comparing the composition of the Earth's atmosphere with that of other planets, James Lovelock developed the Gaia hypothesis—the notion that the Earth behaves as a living organism. The atmospheric gases are out of equilibrium on our planet. The atmosphere was created and is continuously evolved by life, and especially by the green plants which produce free oxygen.

The atmosphere functions much like the roof of your home, keeping out very high-energy radiation (gamma rays, X-rays and ultraviolet) and most of the meteorites which bombard the outer atmosphere. The atmosphere is more transparent to the portion of the electromagnetic spectrum which our bodies are sensitive to—the ultraviolet radiation which tans or burns our skin, the visible light we use to see, and the infrared radiation which warms us. Gases in the lower atmosphere function as the glass in a window does, keeping in some of the heat.

Everything is connected to everything else. This basic law of ecology is nowhere more evident than in the atmosphere. All the plants and animals on Earth exist in or depend upon this ocean of air, which extends into our lungs and every green leaf. Gases added to the atmosphere can affect

74

all life on our planet.

The high-energy life-style of humans now adds gases to the atmosphere at an alarming rate. The average American dumps 5 tons of carbon into the atmosphere each year, 5 times the average of one ton for every human in the biosphere. Methane, oxides of nitrogen and other gases, in addition to carbon dioxide, remain in the lower atmosphere and trap more heat. This is like adding extra insulation to your house without turning down the heat. At the same time, chlorine-containing compounds make their way to the upper atmosphere where they destroy the ozone layer. This then allows in more high-energy radiation. This is analogous to punching holes in the roof of your house, except, instead of getting wet, we get cancer.

Timid proposals developed in the realms of economics and short-term politics won't solve these global problems. The players in these games are locked in the "Think locally—Act globally" dictates of the bottom line or re-election.

Our quality of life is directly connected to an understanding of the natural world and the physical processes upon which our lives depend.

Consumption
April 23 & 24, 1993

For too long we've been told by economists and politicians that it's up to us to consume our way out of recession. If consumer confidence rises, we're told, then we'll spend more money and be on the road to recovery. The message simply stated is—"Consume more."

There are *at least* two problems with this approach. They relate to quantity and to quality.

First we should ask if we really need to consume more? Statistics indicate that our country already consumes much more than its fair share of the Earth's resources. The World Health Organization estimates that on our planet, over 35,000 children die each day, many from hunger and malnutrition. In contrast, a survey last year found that 66 percent of Americans are over their recommended weight range. With just 5 percent of the world's people, we consume about 25 percent of the world's oil, aluminum, lead and mercury, and over 50 percent of the aluminum cans. Per capita, Americans produce more waste than any other country and use more energy than any country except Canada and the Persian Gulf nations. We consume over 3 billion pounds of plastic bottles and produce nearly 500 billion pounds of garbage each year. Like an overweight human staring at a plate of sugar-drenched donuts, consuming more may not be the most intelligent strategy for us.

Let's compare the situation to something with which we're very familiar—our own bodies. We know that if we consume more calories than we use, our weight increases. As our weight increases, we need even more food energy to move around and to maintain this greater weight. Very few people believe that we'll be better off if we consume more calories. Most studies indicate that in general, people within their recommended weight ranges are healthier.

What we consume also matters. A given number of calories from whole grains, vegetables and fruits will have a different effect on our body than that same number of calories from meat, refined and processed foods, artificial sweeteners and fats.

One indication of the idiocy of economics is that it adds up cigarette sales and advertising costs, medical expenses for cancer treatment, sales of toxic chemicals, cleanup costs for radioactive wastes, and gun and pornography sales right along with the cost of children's immunizations, sales of books and garden seeds, day-care expenses, and librarians' and teachers' salaries, to find out how we are doing and how high our gross domestic product is. The bigger the number, the better. Now you see why they call it gross.

Can you imagine adding those things and the value of all other domestic goods and services together, and then judging success by the percentage that number goes up each year. That's economics for you.

This kind of accounting gives greater value to lettuce shipped in from California than to lettuce grown in our garden. It values extensive medical treatment more than wellness achieved by a healthy life-style as well as small throwaway packages over home production. Our economic system gives the nod almost every time to complicated, roundabout ways of satisfying our needs in its striving for bigger numbers.

We humans, however, have other dimensions—other senses and intelligences. Quality *does* matter. For our personal health, study after study has shown that what we eat is important. Whole grains, vegetables and fruits not only have fewer calories than many processed and refined foods, they also contain a rich mixture of beneficial substances with which we have evolved.

Our direct, personal experience suggests the lunacy of the continued dominance of economic thinking.

This Earth Day, begin to break away from economics. Consume better and consume less. Plant some vegetable seeds in the Earth. Help make the numbers smaller and your life richer.

Earth-Day Soil I
April 24 & 25, 1992

Fertile soil is one of the most essential elements for life on Earth. Its destruction was responsible for the decline of the Mesopotamian, Persian and Roman civilizations. In more recent times, closer to home, the destruction of fertile soil contributed to the Great Depression.

A just-released report from the United Nations found that within the lifetimes of many of us, 11 percent of the Earth's vegetated soils have been significantly damaged. Twenty-four billion tons of topsoil are lost worldwide each year as the human population grows. For each new person to feed, we have 260 tons less topsoil.

To understand what we are losing, let's journey into the good organic soil in our garden. Here is a whole ecosystem in which a vast number of living organisms use minerals, organic matter, sunlight, air and water to create an environment which nourishes the plants which nourish us.

Green and blue-green algae and some bacteria perform photosynthesis, using the sun's energy to turn carbon dioxide into carbohydrates, adding organic matter to the soil. Other bacteria and algae convert the most plentiful component of the atmosphere, nitrogen, into the form plants use as a major nutrient. *Actinomycetes* bacteria and many kinds of fungi consume organic matter and create humus, that near magical substance that results from the healthy aerobic, biological decomposition of organic matter. *Rhizobia* bacteria live in a symbiotic relationship with the roots of legumes such as peas, beans or clover. They extract nitrogen from the air and exchange it for carbohydrates produced by the legumes. Still other bacteria break down organic matter, or carry out key steps in the nitrogen cycle.

The bacteria are so numerous that $\frac{1}{2}$ teaspoon of good soil can contain billions of them, as well as millions of *actinomycetes* and fungi, and 100,000 algae. There are also tiny animals, thousands of protozoa, rotifers, and nematodes. All this in one gram of soil—about $\frac{1}{2}$ teaspoonful.

Insects such as ants, beetles, centipedes, springtails, spiders, sow bugs, mites and millipedes aerate and mix the soil as they feed on organic matter and other living things. Earthworms travel through the soil, aerating it while feeding and leaving behind a trail of their very fertile castings. The web of life is so balanced and interdependent that it is very unlikely that any disease organism or insect pest will become a problem.

Given enough organic matter, such as plant residues or compost, and minerals (including calcium), this complex ecosystem is continuously at work collecting and storing solar energy, feasting on organic matter, cycling minerals, creating humus, and exchanging gases and nutrients with plant roots.

Humus, created by this ecosystem, acts like a sponge to hold water and creates a crumb structure in the soil which allows air and plant roots to penetrate easily. Humus helps a sandy soil to hold water and a clay soil to drain. It is a reservoir of nutrition.

Plants send their roots through the soil, sometimes many feet down, opening up additional passageways, bringing up fresh minerals from the deeper layers of soil, and creating a zone of extraordinary biological activity (the rhizosphere) around each root. Carbon dioxide and hydrogen given off by the roots increase the acidity nearby and help release nutrients held by the humus and clay particles.

A slightly acid soil (with a pH near neutral) will encourage soil organisms and their processing of organic matter helps maintain that condition. Compaction by machines or feet, and excessive rototilling can be as harmful to soil life as tornadoes or earthquakes are to ours. Chemical fertilizers are harsh materials which tend to make the soil more acid and destroy organic matter. Toxic pesticides devastate the microscopic life of the soil.

We can't begin to care for the world's soils if we don't

each care for the soil in our own yard. In the diversity, ecological complexity, and health of good garden soil, we find an important model for our larger-scale relationships to the Earth.

Earth Day Soil II
May 1 & 2, 1992

S pring's here with dreams of delicious vegetables, fragrant flowers, and the promise of luxuriant shade on summer days. Time to stop at the garden center for a little limestone and to check out the seeds. Just inside the front door, oh what an awful smell. Our nostrils are assaulted by the strong chemical odor of pesticides and synthetic, energy-intensive fertilizers. Dreams are brought crashing down on the commercial altar of 4-step lawn care.

Store owners say they'd be out of business without the profits from spring sales of the 4-step lawn programs. Unfortunately, *with* their continued use, our soil, our dogs, and Long Island Sound may be out of business.

We need to know a little about soil to understand how senseless and harmful these chemical programs are. A good soil, the soil found in the woods, or under an organic lawn or garden, is alive with billions of living things in each handful. These range from microscopic algae and bacteria, to earthworms and sow bugs. The soil is a complex ecosystem in which living things produce humus and fertility from organic matter, mineral particles, air and water.

The more organic matter and humus in the soil, the better its structure. A lawn grown on this kind of soil, with a near neutral pH, needs to be fertilized only once a year, in the early fall. This is especially true if grass clippings are left to become food for the living things in the soil. A little clover in the lawn will further reduce the need for nitrogen fertilizer.

If you were looking for the best way to destroy this elegant soil ecosystem, it would be hard to find anything short of a bomb or a bulldozer which would do as much harm as these 4-step programs. Each of the 4 steps includes a high-nitrogen fertilizer which literally burns up the organic matter in the soil, removing it as structure and food for essential organisms. It also stimulates growth, which creates the need for more cutting and watering, and encourages thatch. Much of the nitrogen leaches out, eventually finding its way to Long Island Sound or to inland lakes, where it stimulates the excessive growth that causes eutrophication and death for these bodies of water. As more chemical nitrogen is applied, more humus and organic matter are destroyed. This destruction lessens the soil's ability to hold nitrogen and water in reserve for the grass. Chemical fertilizers tend to create acid conditions which discourage much of the soil's life.

The 4 steps usually include 2 kinds of herbicides and at least one insecticide over the course of the year. Imagine the combined effects of these 3 or 4 toxic chemicals on those billions of living things in each handful of your soil. This occurs, of course, after you've destroyed the organic matter which provides their food and homes. It mirrors the tactics from the Vietnam War. Burn the village and then kill its inhabitants. Not only the tactics, but also the chemicals from that war are used. The most widely sold lawn herbicide, 2,4-D, is half of Agent Orange. This poison, besides killing most food plants, also kills clover, which creates the need for more fertilizers to replace the nitrogen formerly provided by the clover. Those clever chemical companies.

And what about your dog? Recent research shows that dogs whose owners used 2,4-D on their lawns have a 30 percent increase in malignant lymphoma. This disease is the canine equivalent of non-Hodgkin's lymphoma which has been connected to farmers' use of this same herbicide. The risk to dogs is increased to 90 percent if the homeowners applied the 2,4-D themselves. Amateurs are often more zealous than professionals when they apply chemicals.

Like addictive drugs, once you've been on the 4-step lawn program, dependency develops. It is easy to destroy the life and humus in your soil with chemicals. It is much harder to rebuild it. However, with limestone and compost, time and understanding, you can restore a chemically-damaged soil. This will result in a healthier, more resilient and less artificial-looking lawn. It will save you money and help our environment.

Solar-Powered Air Conditioners
May 3 & 4, 1991

Trees are quiet, solar-powered air conditioners. On the next warm, sunny day, walk from an open field or parking lot into a grove of trees. You will discover what scientific studies in many parts of the country have found: Trees cool the environment.

Remember those very balmy days in March? The sun was at the same angle it is in late September and the Earth was cooler. Yet it seemed very hot, because the deciduous trees had not yet leafed out.

Trees cool the environment in at least 3 ways:
1. They absorb solar energy and store it as molecular bonds in leaves and wood.
2. They transpire water which, as anyone who has stood wet and naked in the breeze knows, has a cooling effect.
3. They provide shade and create temperature differentials which can encourage breezes.

They do all this while cleaning the air, protecting the soil, and providing homes, foods and fuel for many of nature's creatures.

Every spring we are encouraged to buy electric air conditioners. These non-solar appliances use motors, compressors, and fans, all of which consume energy and make noise. They require coolant chemicals, many of which destroy the ozone layer and worsen the greenhouse effect.

We can get electricity for these air conditioners by splitting atoms, which ensures that electricity will continue to become more expensive, and we will have increasing amounts of radioactive wastes to store in our own or someone else's backyard. Or we can get electricity from burning oil, coal, natural gas or garbage. All of these cause air pollution, worsen the greenhouse effect, and are more expensive.

We can also generate electricity using dammed water. Because electric air-conditioning requires so much energy, the only way to get enough is to build enormous new hydroelectric projects like the one planned for James Bay in northern Canada. This will flood an area the size of France, making refugees of millions of innocent people and animals, while it drowns billions of important plants. Our landscape will be scarred with high voltage power lines which bring the electricity from there to here.

And how do electric, *non*-solar air conditioners work? They move heat from the inside to the outside, making life cooler for some and hotter for others. But aside from the heat moved, electric air conditioners are significant sources of heat themselves. All the energy used to turn motors, fans and compressors ends up in the environment as waste heat. And the sad tale doesn't end here. In order to make the electricity, 2 to 3 times as much energy is wasted as heat at the power plant, which warms the air and water directly.

If we continue to build glass office towers with sealed windows and malls and apartments surrounded by asphalt, we are doomed to a growing dependency on the world's energy giants. These are the companies which think that solar air-conditioning means using expensive, high-tech windmills, photovoltaic cells and concentrating collectors. These produce electricity that is fed to the grid and sold to us to use in our electric air conditioners which have been manufactured by the military-industrial complex.

Do we want a future filled with nuclear power plants and radioactive waste sites, a future of oil spills, oil shocks and oil wars, a future with huge areas flooded in sensitive Arctic regions and high-voltage transmission lines—or a future filled with trees and buildings which are sized and shaped to be cooled by natural processes?

Trees are quiet, solar-powered air conditioners, and evergreen trees planted to the northwest will also keep your house warmer in the winter.

The School Freezer
May 8 & 9, 1992

I think many of us have the feeling that our government has evolved from a solution to our common problems into a major source of those problems, creating a vast gulf between our individual and our collective best interests. This gulf has been filled by large corporations and local bureaucracies which are destructive to both the individual and the collective good.

For example, the federal government gives us the choice of buying a Seawolf Submarine (which we probably don't need) or seeing our fellow citizens laid off at Electric Boat. And consider Connecticut farmers, whose federal tax dollars have been used for years to subsidize irrigation projects, and roads and fuels for long-distance trucking, which benefited California farmers and hurt Connecticut ones. A nearby school provides another clear example.

One recent evening, I gave a gardening presentation in the cafeteria of a small neighborhood elementary school in Bridgeport. Since a kitchen is the most basic and important science laboratory, I looked around. This one was very clean. In fact it was vacuously neat, full of stainless steel and the hum of powerful electric motors. One 12-foot long wall contained a walk-in cooler and a deep walk-in freezer. The cooler was locked, but when I opened the freezer (with a minus 8 degree Fahrenheit reading on its thermometer) I found just two or three dozen small boxed pizzas, several bags of hard rolls, a couple of other items and mostly a lot of very cold emptiness. Less than 5 percent of its over 500 cubic feet of below-zero space was filled.

Besides the large, locked walk-in cooler, a cooler on wheels for milk was humming away, too. There was no stove. Food prepared from taxpayer-funded farm surpluses is brought in daily to this feeding station, heated as needed in a high-tech, specialized food warmer.

Creating cold takes a lot of electricity and in Bridgeport, electricity costs are among the highest in the country.

Bridgeport taxpayers not only buy electricity to run an essentially empty freezer, they also buy the fuel to make that electricity. Here's how this works. Every day the custodian puts a plastic bag inside two small garbage cans in each classroom, and a heavy-duty bag inside each of a dozen or more large garbage cans. That amounts to thousands of plastic bags each year for just this one small school. Every day, these bags and their contents of junk food and candy wrappers, small plastic sugar-water containers and about 300 individual lunch packages (often including aluminum food trays) plus the usual debris from a school are thrown away. The school system pays to have its trash hauled to Bridgeport's garbage-burning facility, where it pays an additional $62 per ton to have it turned into electricity.

Meanwhile, this school district's administration is worried that if they buy real books, i.e., low-cost paperbacks instead of expensive, dull and ineffective basal readers, some children might take them home and keep them. Can you believe that a school system is willing to buy and pay to throw away dozens of plastic bags every day in every school, but is unwilling to give books to children?

This school has recently had the school secretary and part-time school nurse furloughed, but the electric utility, plastic bag makers, and trash haulers and burners continue to get paid.

The parent-teacher organization there has raised money, most of it from the students' families, to buy a copy machine and playground equipment for the school. Yet these parents see their city, state, and federal taxes soar to pay not only for plastic bags, wasted electricity, fancy kitchen equipment and garbage disposal, but also for subsidies and tax benefits to oil producers, incinerator builders, enormous dairy farms and chemical manufacturers.

Although we all know that plastic bags and empty freezers are less important for the educational process than books and a nurse, the maze of bureaucracies and state and federal regulations implies the opposite.

How can we expect intelligence from the students when the school system itself is so unintelligent?

Prenatal Care
May 10 & 11, 1991

For over a year there has been a disturbing presence in our landscape: prominent billboards featuring sleazy looking cartoon camels at play with fast cars, boats, or women. Their purpose is to sell cigarettes, the delivery system for a very addictive and health-destroying drug, nicotine. Like most parents and ex-smokers, I fervently hope my son doesn't start smoking. Like most aware people, I realize what a large strain smoking-related diseases place on our already overburdened health-care system.

At a time when libraries and parks are being closed, teachers are being laid off, and tens of thousands of expectant mothers don't get enough or any prenatal care, I wondered how our society can spend resources and employ people to advertise cigarettes. The answer is that, if this cigarette maker didn't use the money to buy advertising, it would have to pay taxes on the money instead. Because it doesn't pay taxes on that money (taxes which could be used to finance more care for expectant mothers), either clinics close, or our taxes go up, or both.

Last weekend, though, a fuller picture of what is going on emerged. This situation demonstrates a tension and contradiction between our economic system and our society's health. In our economic system, the only value is a high rate of return on investment. In our society, we have other values that relate to the well-being and happiness of people.

It turns out that much of the money for the recent leveraged buy-out of this tobacco giant, RJR Nabisco, came from state pension funds in New York, Massachusetts, and 9 other states. The pension funds are state tax money which is set aside to provide retirement benefits to state employees.

Investment in the tobacco giant means that the financial health in retirement of today's state workers is directly dependent on the financial health of the second largest cigarette maker in the world. The more cigarettes sold, the more profits and the better return to the pension fund. However, the more cigarettes sold, the more smoking-related illnesses that need to be treated within our health-care system. This then increases the cost of insurance for those who can pay, and the cost of state assistance to the growing number of those who can't.

But, you might argue, cigarette sales are declining in this country. The real growth market is overseas. If it is good for our retirement funds, do we care if people overseas get lung cancer, emphysema, and all the other well-documented diseases related to smoking cigarettes?

To be fair, at the time the pension funds were invested, RJR Nabisco was also the second largest marketer of distilled spirits (liquor) and the country's largest seller of fried chicken. Although it is hard to trace all the connections in the "Let's make a deal" maze of privately-held corporations, it seems that its major business now, besides tobacco, is food, including packaged and sugary foods, as well as tropical fruits. However, 80 percent of operating profits in the recent quarter came from cigarette sales.

Like many of the most profitable businesses, including oil, chemicals, and alcohol, cigarettes look like a good investment because economics has a very narrow view—the bottom line in this quarter or fiscal year, or the rate of growth. Many of the greatest costs (e.g. personal and environmental illness) are postponed to the future and dumped on the general taxpayers. Meanwhile the large corporations use all the tax system's loopholes to avoid paying their taxes.

Connections are very important. By connecting the financial health of retirement plans with increasing sales of cigarettes which cause physical illness, the financial dealmakers have put us in a no-win situation.

Energy and Matter
May 8 & 9, 1992

Energy and matter are the building blocks of the universe, and are neither created nor destroyed. The equation $E = mc^2$ expresses their equivalence, but on Earth, except in nuclear reactors or weapons, energy and matter remain distinct and separate.

This separateness is important because energy and matter behave quite differently. Although the atoms which make up matter can be recycled again and again without losing their usefulness, when we use energy, we degrade it and make it less useful. This creates a quantity of entropy or disorder in the universe.

This distinctive behavior is the same whether we are talking about the formation of the solar system, or the growth of broccoli in our garden.

Since the latter is easier to look at, let's examine the growth of broccoli. Like all green plants, it is able to capture solar energy and store some of it in chemical bonds between carbon atoms.

Sunlight is very high-quality energy. It allows us to see, powers photosynthesis, creates heat inside a greenhouse, and can be converted into electricity by a photovoltaic cell. Yet, once it falls on the broccoli plant it becomes less useful; some is reflected, some is converted to heat and a little is stored as food energy in the plant. None of this energy, however, has the high quality of sunlight. Although it can produce a certain heat in our bodies as we digest the broccoli, this energy can no longer power photosynthesis.

From hydrogen atoms fusing into helium in the sun (releasing radiant energy at 5,500 degrees Celsius) to digestion releasing food energy from broccoli at human body temperature, energy is flowing downhill, becoming less useful, ending up as waste heat headed toward the minus 270 degree temperature of space.

Let's contrast this with the matter in broccoli. About 44 percent of its dry weight is carbon. It is by joining carbon atoms together to produce sugars that broccoli or any other green plant is able to store solar energy. The carbon that the broccoli uses is taken in from the atmosphere as carbon dioxide, which probably came from exhaust gases. These gases may be the result of our body's breaking down of the energy containing carbohydrates in our last meal, or the result of our car's breaking down of the hydrocarbons in gasoline—solar

89

energy stored by green plants millions of years ago. In either case, that carbon atom has been a part of many different plants and animals and has assumed many forms in its life on Earth. Carbon was originally created from simpler elements in the explosion of a supernova billions of years ago, and will keep cycling from plant, to animal, to atmosphere, and then back to plants for years to come.

Although all the information we have suggests that this continual cycling of matter and the downhill flow of energy (which creates disorder) are universal principles, in recent times our society has behaved as if the opposite were true. We have found as many ways as possible to use energy and have tried to throw matter away.

Think of the fossil and nuclear energy we use to grow, ship, process, wrap and market our food. Frozen, packaged, ready-to-eat, distant-grown food often consumes 30 times as much fossil and nuclear energy as the solar energy it contains. Yet our bodies can use only the stored solar energy in that food. This large consumption of non-solar energy increases the cost of, and the pollution from, our food, as well as the disorder or entropy on Earth.

This is the reason that a hand-tended organic garden, combined with a compost pile, makes so much sense. Although it is small-scale and very local, it embodies and respects the laws of the universe. The garden efficiently manages the flow of solar energy from the sun to plants and eventually to ourselves as it minimizes polluting energies and recycles organic matter.

Planting Trees
May 17 & 18, 1991

L ike making compost and growing vegetables, planting trees is an activity which is important to the health of our future. As many of us as possible should understand how to choose and plant a tree.

And, like activities from playing sports to starting a family, there are three steps which will help ensure success: intelligent planning, careful execution, and a commitment to follow-through.

For the health of the tree and for maximum aesthetic and environmental effect, a tree should be appropriate for the soil, moisture, light and space available, and should relate well for years to come to nearby plantings, buildings and power lines.

Trees like dogwood, *Oxydendrum* and Japanese maples grow slowly, tolerate shade and are fairly small at maturity. In contrast, hemlocks, pines and oaks, once established, can grow very rapidly and reach over 100 feet tall. In the winter, pines and hemlocks will create a warmer area to the south and a colder, shady zone on their north side.

Maples have shallow, fibrous root systems which limit the ability of plants to grow under them, while oaks have deeper roots, so shrubs or small trees near them will grow well.

The pioneer species like black locust and eastern redcedar need full sun and are adaptable to undeveloped soils. The great trees of the climax forest—sugar maples, beeches, and hemlocks—need lots of room for their roots and branches to spread and are tolerant of shade.

Apples, cherries, chestnuts and walnuts will provide food for us, while the redcedar is used by 75 species of birds for food or shelter.

Aspen trees grow on dry rocky uplands and red maples grow in rich, moist swamps. The honeylocust is tolerant of urban pollution and casts a light, dappled shade, while the Norway maple, also tolerant of pollution, casts a very dense shade and can become a weed. Since dogwoods like to grow in open shade in rich forest soils, it shouldn't be surprising that they are prone to disease when planted in full sun, in the middle of a chemically-maintained lawn, and nicked regularly by lawnmowers.

Probably the most significant recent discovery about trees concerns their root system. For almost all trees, their root systems are shallower than was previously thought and extend out from the trunk much farther, in many cases well beyond the drip line.

For this reason, when planting trees, loosen the soil to the depth of the root ball in a circle 3 to 5 times the diameter of the root ball. Then dig a hole in the center—the same depth as the root ball and slightly larger. Remove any plastic burlap or strings which are around the root ball, and cut and remove the wire basket if one is present. Any plastic or the metal basket left in the hole can girdle the roots sooner or later. Place the tree in the hole, add enough soil to help hold it straight, and then fold down into the hole the biodegradable burlap which wrapped the ball. Finish filling the hole with dirt, using water rather than your foot to settle it.

The tree should be planted at the same depth it was growing in the nursery, unless the site is poorly drained, in which case it can be just a few inches higher. If the tree is planted lower, the roots may not get enough oxygen.

Trees should be staked only if absolutely necessary, and any wrappings or tags should always be removed.

Three to five inches of mulch spread over the area of loosened soil, and an inch of water, per week, through the fall, complete a first year's follow-through.

As sources of beauty and cooling, food and building materials, clean air and fertile soil, trees are hard to beat. Plant some soon.

Saving Seeds
May 22 & 23, 1992

One of the great pleasures each spring is experiencing the high germination rate and vigor of seeds we've saved from vegetables grown in the previous year's garden.

This spring, it was the cayenne pepper seeds Suzanne had saved as she was cooking supper one night. She selected a good quality ripe pepper, with appropriate heat, dried the seeds on the counter for a few days, and stored them in an envelope in a cool dry place until this March. Then I planted them, as well as several other kinds of hot peppers from commercial sources and seeds from some dried ancho peppers we had bought to cook with. The germination varied widely, from not at all for the peppers bought as food, to rapid and complete for the cayenne from our garden. Seeds we had saved from basil and an heirloom paste tomato also germinated vigorously.

It shouldn't be surprising that local seeds germinate better. Seeds are living things. Like all life they respond to care and to treatment in keeping with their long evolutionary history.

Saving seeds establishes a continuity in our garden from year to year. We know these seeds do well here. It is also consistent with what humans have done for millennia, selecting the hardiest, tastiest, most prolific, or best all-around food plant, and saving its seeds for planting the next year. In this way, over thousands of years, wild grasses have evolved with humans to become the wheat, rice, corn and other grains on which we depend.

Before you begin to save your own seeds, it might be helpful to review some plant-reproduction basics.

We should be aware of the sexual activities, i.e. pollination habits, of the plants whose seeds we want to save, and we need to understand the changes modern science and commerce have made in some seeds.

Plants like tomatoes, peppers, beans and peas are self-pollinating. That means the fertilization process takes place within each flower; the pollen travels only the short distance from the stamen to the stigma.

Other plants, like corn and squash, are cross-pollinating. Insects or wind must carry the pollen from a stamen in one flower to the stigma of another flower on the same or a different plant. For example, pollen from a summer squash plant could be carried by a bee to a nearby acorn squash plant. The fruit resulting from that pollination will be an acorn squash. But if its seeds are planted, the next generation of fruit probably will resemble neither the acorn nor the summer squash.

Vegetables such as cabbage, carrots, parsley and beets are biennials and produce seed only in the second year. Dill and coriander are close relatives of carrots and parsley, but they produce seeds so well the first season, that they seed themselves in our garden almost every year.

So far I've described the open pollination process. Some seeds are hybrid, the result of human-mediated fertilization between two very different parents. For example, an inbred line of sweet cherry tomatoes may be crossed with an inbred large, but flavorless tomato to produce large tasty hybrid tomatoes like Big Boy and Beefeater. Seeds saved from a hybrid tomato will very likely not produce anything like the fruit they came from; they will revert to some other combination of their grandparents' characteristics.

Hybrid seeds usually produce plants with great vigor and uniformity. However, you have to go to the seed company each year to buy new seeds. Since much of the hybridizing is done for large-scale commercial growers, characteristics of hybrid vegetables may be things like uniform ripening in a short period, or ability to tolerate machine harvesting, or resistance to injury in shipping—traits which are irrelevant in a home garden where a long season of production and flavor are much more important.

Many seed companies have been bought up by multinational drug, chemical and energy corporations. To them, the need for their products is a desirable trait in seeds and for farmers, so they breed and select for that need. These large-scale programs affect the diversity and genetic resources of our planet negatively.

By saving our own seeds, we can counter this trend, save money and help to preserve genetic diversity. We'll also simultaneously be learning about the sex habits of our vegetables.

May Garden Report
May 24 & 25, 1991

Ah, the pleasures of the garden in May. Early light, long evenings and the rapid growth of vegetables, flowers, trees and baby chickens make May an exciting and vibrant time.

Almost everything can be planted in May: seeds of lettuce, carrots, beets, turnips, chard and spinach. After the middle of the month, frost-sensitive squash, beans and corn, the "three sisters" of the Native Americans, can be planted. As the soil continues to warm, and frost-free nights arrive, transplants of tomatoes, eggplants and peppers are set out.

Ah, the pleasures of the garden in May: flowers, fragrances and first fruits combine for such wonderful pleasure. To share the joys and work with children and a loved one is bliss.

Vegetable perennials, like asparagus and rhubarb and annual greens like arugula, lettuce, turnip tops and spinach, are all ready to eat. These greens, sown on March 26, were big and delicious last weekend. The Winter Density romaine lettuce is beautiful and tasty. Snowflake peas planted on St. Patrick's Day were big enough to eat on May 18th. Garlic greens and dill provide flavor for savory dishes. Strawberries swell and redden, and the flowers on the raspberries, dewberries and blackberries promise fruit for the next several months.

The alpine goat, Princess Leah, took a ride to New Haven to join the small farm that students from High School in the Community are creating as part of an intensive Ecology course, now in its ninth year. A pig, chickens and a rabbit complete their barnyard, next to the compost piles and the raised-bed gardens. Many students are truly engaged in learning for the first time in their school careers by the real life lessons on the farm.

Back at our farm, the baby chicks love the fresh picked chickweed, eating the leaves and seeds and pecking at the dirt between the roots for tasty mineral and protein morsels.

Madam Duck sits on a nest of 7 eggs, a masterful construction of feathers, weeds and leaves. Daddy Duck stays close by, except for occasional excursions to the small metal pond, to find food under the leaf mulch around the azaleas, or down to the garden for a taste of spinach.

And speaking of spinach, as she was preparing dinner recently, Suzanne passed a handful of young spinach leaves beneath my nose. The wonderful aroma lingered in my mind for days. The definite difference in homegrown foods is that they really have flavor. Eggs from the backyard flock are delicious, while store-bought eggs just taste like eggs. I recently realized why, growing up without a garden in the suburban 1950s, I only liked tomatoes when we visited Uncle Bill's upstate New York farm. It was one of the few opportunities I had to eat tomatoes that grew nearby.

And oh, the fragrances of May: *carlesii* viburnums, Marie Hoffman azaleas, lilacs, and lilies of the valley, giving way to fragrant zones around the Rugosa rose clumps, the drifts of irises and now the peonies.

Recent research shows the important role that smell and odor play in the bonding between mother and child. Strong artificial smells can interfere. Most of us have some very evocative olfactory relationships with plants which can take us instantly back in time, or perhaps to a peaceful place.

With a different vision of our relationship to the Earth, we could replace our ribbons of diesel fumes, our stinking mounds of garbage piling up near most major cities, and our smelly chemical plants with the fragrances of the plant world, as we turn our surplus corn into fuel for efficient mass transit, attack the earth with fewer powerful machines, and fulfill our most important needs close to home.

Cynthia and the Carpenter Bees
May 29 & 30, 1992

There was a message from Cynthia on our machine. "Big bees are flying around our house. What should I do?" Then, as if to make sure I would call back, she added "Should I go to the hardware store and get a poison spray?"

That week in early May I'd noticed large carpenter bees flying around the eaves of our house and several other buildings. I returned Cynthia's call and asked a few questions to be sure that she actually did have carpenter bees. They were making perfect round holes, just under $1/2$ inch diameter in bare wood under the eaves. The bees were an inch or so long, shiny on top with a smooth abdomen. Yes, they were definitely carpenter bees. No, she shouldn't get some poison.

I told her, half jokingly, that she should watch them for several weeks to see what they do. They were probably just looking for a place to settle down and raise a family in peace. This seemed reasonable. Although I was being flip at the time, it was close to the truth.

By the time she realized I was joking, I had found my reference, "The Least Toxic Control Manual for Wood-Boring Insects."

The first control strategy was to protect the carpenter bees. They are very important for pollination and are harmless to people. The males can't sting and the females don't sting, but will bite if they are handled roughly. When Cynthia called, the young adults (having spent the winter in holes in houses or trees) were emerging, breeding, defending territory, and making nests for this year's eggs. The males are most noticeable as they defend their territory or challenge another male's territory. Meanwhile, the females go about the work of provisioning their nests with a mixture of pollen and nectar to nourish the young bees when they hatch. Sound familiar? It is while gathering these materials that the female carpenter bee pollinates flowers. She will lay up to 6 eggs in her 4 to 6 inch gallery in the wood. Each egg is closed in a cell with its food.

Now, after a couple of weeks of intense activity, the bees are much less evident. In August, young adults will emerge, and the males will vigorously defend their territory, but will put off mating until about the same time next spring.

There are several other strategies for control. Carpenter bees like unpainted wood, especially softwoods such as white and southern yellow pine, California redwood, cedar, Douglas fir and cypress. Using other kinds of wood, or keeping the wood painted or varnished, discourages carpenter bees. They usually do not build their nests in structural wood, and in any case, their tunneling is slow. If you want to discourage reuse of an existing tunnel, a bit of steel wool in the hole with screening stapled over it will do.

If you absolutely must kill these useful and gentle creatures, use a pyrethrum-based insecticide. This is relatively non-toxic to mammals and breaks down quickly.

The more I learn about the way the Earth works, the more I respect the role of insects in it. Most of us are aware of honeybees' role in pollinating fruit and vegetable plants, but it was what I learned about wasps and hornets which really impressed me. Wasps come in a variety of sizes. Many of them are very important predators of pests in the garden.

Hornets are predators of yellow jackets and flies. Most insects would rather take care of their own business, which is often useful to us, than bother us. The vast majority of insects are beneficial. As we learn more about them, our appreciation for the elegance of nature increases.

As I was finishing this piece, a book I had ordered arrived: *Common Sense Pest Control* by William and Helga Olkowski and Sheila Daar. Published by Taunton Press in Newtown, Connecticut, it is a deep reservoir of information to help us appreciate and manage the insects and other pests with whom we share our planet.

The Convenience Store
June 5 & 6, 1992

One piece of information stood out from the rhetoric swirling around South Central Los Angeles soon after the disturbances there. It was the large number of gas and food convenience outlets one major oil company, ARCO, owned in that area. It had over 50 stores, many of which were damaged or looted. All will be rebuilt.

A friend thought that it was admirable that this company did business in such a distressed area. That may be, but I questioned the effect of one large corporation taking money out of the community with such a sizable herd of cash cows. Besides gas, these stores sell junk food, soda, cigarettes and many other ways to ruin human health. Frequently convenience means paying a higher price. How could there be so many of these stores in such a poor community?

It was jarring, but shouldn't have been. Convenience stores can be seen as the embodiment of the kinds of economic relationships which impoverish not only South

Central Los Angeles, but also South and Central America—not just small towns in New England, but also villages in Africa. They impoverish both our environment and our spirit. These economic relationships grow out of linear-mechanical thinking, cheap energy, and centralized control. They thrive on the flow of money out of communities in return for a steady input of almost all of life's necessities. Many of these essentials travel long distances over circuitous routes. For the community, these relationships create large amounts of waste which range from auto pollution to candy wrappers and soda bottles, as they leave a wake of health and social problems.

This is how it works. Potatoes, wheat and corn (which are cheap and plentiful from subsidized corporate farms in a decaying and underpopulated countryside) are turned into salt, sugar, fat, and often chemical-laden, branded, snack foods (which are sold in decaying and overpopulated urban areas at per pound prices higher than the finest, humanely-raised organic chicken).

Carbonated water is laced with sweeteners (from the chemical plant or giant farm) and with caffeine or cola (from the destructive export agriculture of tropical countries) and sold in single-use containers. Energy subsidies and large size ensure that beverage companies can sell the bottle and the drink cheaply enough to drive a local company (which refills its bottles) out of business. Now communities are finding that recycling these bottles costs almost as much as discarding them. In either case, it's a subsidy to the giant bottler.

The income possibilities of large-scale processing, advertising, transporting and retailing ventures are exploited by large corporations, with profits returned to pension plans, insurance companies, and stock portfolios which are outside the financial world of both the rural and urban poor. These are the very folks who are finding that, in the global marketplace, they must compete with workers all over the Earth for the job of providing food, energy and clothing for their own community.

100

And more and more, the suburban middle class, who might someday benefit from these profits because of their pensions and other investments, see their taxes rise not only to subsidize energy, agriculture and tax benefits for this system of long-distance dependency, but also to pay for security forces to protect the system in Los Angeles, Kuwait, and Central America. Not surprisingly, costs for health care, education, and environmental cleanup soar.

In this existing system, the role of people is to get a job to get the money to be good consumers. Production and consumption are separated, often by thousands of miles. The people in South Central Los Angeles and their counterparts in El Salvador, for example, who might have a common interest in changing this system, are separated by great distance but united as consumers by global marketing.

Just as the dismantling of the Los Angeles transit system by the automobile industry earlier in this century created a dependency on cars, the dismantling of local production and sufficiency by the food, biotech, and marketing juggernaut creates both a dependency on its products, and expensive convenience stores.

This dependency is detrimental to local self-reliance everywhere.

Iraq and Bangladesh
June 7 & 8, 1991

Twice already in the year 1991, hundreds of thousands of people have died as the result of a single event. Is there any connection between these two tragedies?

As a result of the Allied Forces storm against Iraq and the cyclone landing on Bangladesh, the immediate effect was

101

over a hundred thousand deaths, with enough dying later from hunger, disease, poor sanitary conditions, homelessness and poverty to bring the total to well over 200,000. To put this in perspective, these deaths in the first 5 months of this year are equivalent to the death of every person in Bridgeport and New Haven and a few of their suburbs.

In the war against Iraq, we unleashed an enormous destructive force using our advanced technology fueled by millions of barrels of petroleum. This countered the actions of Saddam Hussein, who had built up an enormous arsenal of weapons purchased with his oil revenues from members of the United Nations Security Council. The oil reserves in the region paid for and fueled Iraq's military, and were the reason for Hussein's aggression against Kuwait.

Although some deny that the Persian Gulf War was about oil, as someone said, "President Bush would never have spent billions of dollars and put our soldiers at risk if Kuwait were a major exporter of broccoli." Our current economy is dependent on energy and the oil companies depend on keeping oil at a reasonable price so we don't consider switching to alternative sources like solar energy and conservation.

The cyclone that hit Bangladesh also unleashed a tremendous destructive force, which despite its origin in the natural processes of the Earth, may well have been made worse by the same substance which fueled the Gulf conflict—namely, oil, and the industrialized world's voracious consumption of it. Cyclones, like hurricanes, are the Earth's heat-transfer mechanisms, moving vast quantities of heat from the tropics to more northerly latitudes.

We know that we have significantly increased the concentrations of greenhouse gases, like methane, carbon dioxide, and chlorofluorocarbons in the atmosphere, largely as a result of the tremendous energy consumption in the industrialized world. We know that changing the atmosphere changes the energy equation of the Earth which is poised between the 5,500 degrees Celsius energy source of the sun, and the minus 270 degrees Celsius energy sink of outer space.

Although exactly what will happen as we alter the atmosphere is unclear, it seems very likely that the climate will change. Bangladesh has been identified as one of the countries likely to be hardest hit by the consequences of global climate change such as sea-level rise, changing rainfall patterns, and more violent storms.

In order to pursue future wars to secure our access to cheap oil, we are buying Stealth airplanes (at $143 million each) which will use 1,000 or more gallons of fuel per hour to move just one person around. In order to improve the quality of life of Bangladeshis and allow them to better cope with future storms, a recent report suggests that loans of $5 or $10 to individuals and families would make a great difference.

There can never be a peaceful world when a few of the Earth's inhabitants spend billions on weapons of destruction, while the majority of the Earth's inhabitants need just a few dollars to help them meet the basic needs of survival.

The first five months of the year 1991 should be viewed as a warning. If we continue our dependence on fossil fuels and our resource-expensive life styles, we condemn ourselves and our children to ever-rising costs for energy and high-tech weapons. We condemn many more hundreds of thousands of people (mostly poor, Third World inhabitants) to die as a result of the twin effects of the way we live.

Water and the Common Good

June 11 & 12, 1993:

A large stone memorial stands near the docks in Stony Creek, Connecticut. A bit larger than 2 back-to-back soda machines, it is made of the beautiful pink Stony Creek granite which was also used for the base of the Statue of Liberty and the towers of the Brooklyn Bridge. The memorial's sidewalk face contains a drinking fountain for people, and the street side has a large basin for horses and a smaller one near the ground for dogs and other animals. The fountain still works and the basins are full of fresh water.

A similar monument, a few miles west on the New Haven Green, is made of white marble and is taller and wider than the one in Branford but has no basin for horses, and isn't as functional. Pigeons enjoy the full low basins, but both fountains for people are missing. A small trickle of water leaks from a pipe in one empty niche.

However, in near-by stores, anyone who has more than 50¢ can buy a liter or a half-liter of water in a plastic or glass bottle from western Canada, Maine, France or Switzerland.

Water is essential for our existence. We will die in just a few days without a fresh supply, and our bodies need 6 to 8 glasses of water per day. Although we can get this necessary water from juices, milk or other beverages, water itself is best. Because of their diuretic effect, coffee, tea and cola as well as alcoholic beverages, increase water-loss through urination.

What is happening with our drinking water is important. The quality and abundance of the local water supply as well as its beautiful reservoirs, make it a valuable community resource. Our water's low cost is demonstrated by the fact that we flush 40 percent of the drinking water piped into our houses down the toilet with our wastes.

However, the decrease in public drinking fountains and the sale of reservoirs and watersheds, combined with the increase in bottled water sales and water-carrying trucks on the highways, indicate a disturbing trend which raises a few questions.

Does it makes sense to use a polluting, non-renewable resource like diesel fuel to truck water from one place to another, especially if the other place is Connecticut, where we have plentiful, delicious water?

And what about the empty bottles? At current rates it is possible to buy between 2 and 12 gallons of piped-in local water for just what it costs to recycle one small plastic or glass bottle. Even if we don't drink bottled water, our taxes go to subsidize the making of the bottles, their transportation, and their disposal or recycling.

Where else does our money go? The money we spend on bottled water goes to bottle manufacturers, oil companies, and multinational corporations. The profits from our purchase of popular waters from Maine and France go to Nestlé, one of the world's largest food companies, based in Switzerland. Nestlé is the planet's leading supplier of bottled water, and also sells 55 percent of the infant formula in the world.

Selling bottled water and selling infant formula have something in common. Since they are both usually unnecessary and more expensive, customers are won over by being convinced that the local supply is somehow inadequate and that the shipped-in, packaged product is healthier, more convenient, or more chic.

On the other hand, the money we pay to the local water company goes to maintain those very valuable watersheds, reservoirs, treatment plants, and efficient piped-delivery systems which serve the common good in our communities.

But the most important question is: What does this trend say about our society's direction? Community water supplies, like public fountains, provide a public good which is available to all. Trucked-in bottled water provides a private good available to those who can afford it, with a cost to the public for disposal and subsidies, and an outflow of money from the community.

The well-maintained public drinking fountain represents the sense of the common good that we *must* regain if we have any hope of rebuilding our communities.

Mulch
June 12 & 13, 1992

A mulch is a covering for the soil. In nature, except for recently disturbed areas and places like rocky hilltops and sandy shores (where the elements and low fertility keep much from growing), the Earth is not bare.

The soil is covered with plants and the leaves, flowers, seeds, and twigs they drop. In a pine forest, the ground is covered with pine needles. In the mixed hardwood forest, oak and maple leaves cover the soil. In the pasture, the Earth is covered with grass. Grazing or cutting annually prevents trees and shrubs from growing.

There are important reasons for covering the soil.

Bare soil is more subject to erosion by water and wind. Raindrops, containing lots of energy after their long fall, use it to dislodge soil particles, moving the lightest ones, clay and humus. These are the particles which are the most valuable for fertility. Some dislodged particles seal the soil surface, making it harder for water to penetrate. Water then runs off, carrying the very particles which are most important, leaving behind rocks and sand. The blowing soil of the dust bowl years resulted from agricultural practices that left the ground bare for part of the year, and plowed land that should have been left in permanent prairie cover.

A covering of plants and their litter slows raindrops, allowing them to filter into the soil without disturbing it. This would be reason enough to mulch our gardens, but there are others. A mulch of plant materials for the soil acts like clothing for us. It keeps the soil warmer in winter—allowing important soil life to work longer—and moderates summer heat. Billions of soil organisms think they are in a forest rather than in the Sahara. They will be more productive.

There are at least three more reasons for mulching: to conserve moisture, to build fertility and to control weeds. Mulching cuts down on evaporation from the soil, which keeps it more moist and allows nearby plants to thrive. An organic mulch slowly rots into fertility to renew and build topsoil. That is how the soil of this region was created on top of the infertile glacial till left after the last ice age, about 10,000 years ago.

What should we mulch with? Start with what's there. Don't rake leaves away from trees and shrubs. Save yourself the work of raking and mulching by using what nature provides to protect and enrich the soil.

Vegetable gardeners often use straw or hay, both of which are readily available and easy to use. These materials encourage soil life, especially valuable earthworms. Straw, which is what is left after grain is threshed out, has been shown to discourage Colorado potato beetles. Mulch hay may contain seeds which can sprout as weeds in the garden. Whether this is a problem depends on kind and quantity of the seeds. I find it works well to cut tall grass in the fields, clover in the paths or a nearly mature rye cover crop with a scythe for immediate use as garden mulch. This also provides some beneficial nitrogen.

Intensive gardeners keep their plants so close together that they shade the soil, effectively forming a living mulch. Between larger vegetable plants, such as Brussels sprouts and corn, some growers use a living mulch like White Dutch clover which keeps the soil covered and adds nitrogen.

Black plastic as a mulch is sometimes recommended for heat-loving crops like sweet potatoes and melons. It will warm the soil, but cuts down on the liquid and gaseous

107

exchanges between the soil and the air and inevitably presents a disposal problem. In the orient, charred rice hulls are used to warm the soil.

For shrub or perennial gardens where the mulch will remain longer than in vegetable patches, a bark mulch is frequently used. Wood chips will last longer, but may temporarily remove nitrogen from the soil. The larger size of bark nuggets and chips seems less natural. Newer landscape fabrics under a mulch let water and gases pass, but they don't decay, and eventually show through.

There are many benefits to mulching and lots of choices of materials, so keep your soil covered.

Weeds
June 14 & 15, 1991

S ome of the plants which grow in our garden are the ones we planted, and others—frequently much more numerous—are plants that grow on their own, taking advantage of the ecological niche of open soil and fertility that we provide. These are often considered weeds.

For successful gardening, it is useful to know the weeds and their habits. Get a good plant identification book and read, for example, *Stalking the Wild Asparagus* by Euell Gibbons to gain an appreciation of these plants.

Not all weeds are alike. Some weeds, like lamb's-quarters (which indicate fertile soil) and purslane are found in almost every garden and are as tasty and nutritious as many of the vegetables we cultivate. Many weeds like red-root pigweed and ragweed grow very fast and will shade out vegetables like carrots and onions which need lots of light, and grow slowly. Low, slower growing weeds like chickweed or groundsel, growing among corn or pole beans, have little effect except to shade the soil. Weeds like leguminous clover growing in the corn will actually help the corn grow by adding nitrogen to the soil.

Weeds such as the perennial grasses can be hard to pull out, whereas young pigweed and lamb's-quarters pull up very easily. If you leave a piece of the stolon or root of quack grass or mugwort in the ground it will grow a new plant. Mint, a valuable herb, spreads the same way and can become a weed if not contained. Cut off just below the soil line, other weeds will die. And sometimes a weed turns out to be a beautiful and desirable new plant.

Most plants that are considered weeds produce vast quantities of seeds with a very long viability. These seeds sit in the ground just waiting for the right conditions to germinate, grow and reproduce. Cultivation (with a sharp hoe soon after the weed seeds germinate) cuts off the plants and stops most growth. The bigger the weeds get, the more likely that they will compete with flowers and vegetables for sunlight, water and nutrients. The bigger they get, the more likely their root systems will become entangled with the roots of crop plants, making it harder to pull them out without disturbing other established plants. Weeding after a rain is always a good idea.

Chemical control of weeds in the garden with herbicides doesn't work. We want to grow too many different kinds of plants in the garden, and although some vegetables may not be killed by the chemicals, they may be weakened. Plants are too important for our continued existence on this planet for us to risk using chemicals to kill them. And herbicides are probably dangerous to our health.

A good strategy for controlling weeds is to mulch your garden. Traditionally, straw (the stems of grain plants) is used because it is a natural product which is free of weed seeds and breaks down to nourish the soil. Hay is easier to get and works too, although it may introduce undesirable weed and grass seeds into the garden. Grass clippings from a lawn free of herbicides make a good mulch. They are easy to apply because of their fine texture, and they provide some nutrients to the garden as well. Wood chips and sawdust will extract nitrogen from the soil to assist in their decay and may stunt the growth of vegetables. In dry times, the weeds you pull out can be laid on the soil as mulch. Unfortunately, if it rains or you irrigate, some of them will grow again. Any weeds not used this way should be added to the compost pile (unless they have gone to seed) in order to return the nutrients they contain to the soil. All of these mulches encourage beneficial earthworm activity, and allow rain to penetrate. Black plastic mulch is sometimes used, but it is ugly, has disposal problems and doesn't let water penetrate.

Weeds can feed us, nourish and protect our soil, and tell us about its fertility. The more we learn about weeds, the better we can manage them for a more successful garden.

F A L L

S U M M E R

S P R I N G

W I N T E R

Summer Solstice, 1992

June 19 & 20, 1992

It's June, coming up on the Summer Solstice. The peonies are popping open in glorious reds, white and many-petaled pinks. We had our first 'Sugar Snap' peas last night in a stir-fry. Sturdy, breathtaking *catawbiense album* rhododendrons and fragrant Rugosa roses line the way to pick rhubarb for a pie. Suzanne combines its red stalks and just-ripe strawberries with delicious results.

Pale blue and deep purple irises and dark blue lupine blossoms float above verdant spring growth. The tiny flowers on the native raspberries are fertilized and swelling.

Crisp, frilly lettuce in reds and greens grows faster than we can pick it; spinach, arugula, dill, cilantro and oregano are flavorfully abundant.

The sun's altitude is slowly nearing its highest of the year. This is the time of the midnight sun above the Arctic Circle, which for us produces the long twilights which make our cool mornings and fecund evenings so wonderful.

At our home, an overhang on the large south-facing windows keeps the sun out of the house now. These are the same windows which let the low sun shine all the way to the back of the house in the winter. When I told the insurance agent that our house had solar heat, he asked how many panels we had, wrongly believing that if we had solar heat, we must have panels. I told him about the windows, but he still didn't believe me.

Trees to the east and west of our house leafed out quickly in late May. Now they provide cool shade from the hot morning and afternoon sun. Trees are beautiful, quiet, chlorofluorcarbon-free, solar-powered air conditioners. They don't need a nuclear power station or a large dam to work, and they remove carbon dioxide from the air.

The solar clothes dryer we use in the winter is on the protected south side of our house. That area is now in shade,

113

so we've moved the clothesline to the sunny north side, where the garden is. The high angle and long path of the sun make the area north of the house sunny from the spring to the fall equinoxes. This period, from March 20 to September 22 (in 1992) is the primary growing season.

I've just described, and have used for decades, *The Big-Four, Low-Cost, Ready-to-Use Solar Collectors, Designed for a Better Tomorrow*—the garden for food, trees for cooling, south-facing glass for warmth, and a clothesline. They are inexpensive, dependable and widely-available. Like strawberries, rhubarb and the perennial flowers, these solar solutions are long-lasting, pleasant to care for and live with, and easily maintained. They can work as well on a small lot in the city as they do in rural areas, and provide nearly unlimited possibilities for satisfying, productive work.

In contrast, a new, Sunwood development home nearby, given a "Good-Cents" rating by the local electric utility, has only one small window on the south side and no trees to shade the east and west windows from the summer sun.

Building codes require electrical outlets every so many feet along each wall of a house. Although this is supposed to be for the public good, it probably is of more benefit to the banks, insurance companies and appliance manufacturers. The building code contains no requirements for planting shade trees or for orientation to the sun.

As we view the Earth Summit in Rio, and the differences between the developed and developing countries, we realize that, at least since Columbus's visit, western slavery, colonialism, imperialism and corporate greed have pushed native people all over the Earth out of the solar-powered, sustainable lives they have lived for thousands of years, and into crowded urban poverty. The promise of jobs and a western life style has produced not only a disconnection from plants, animals and the sun, but also a world of fast and junk foods, guns, rising taxes and failing educational institutions.

The pleasures of the garden and other solar solutions provide strength and inspiration for the educating and heal-

114

ing we must do. This solstice, let's start creating in our local environments the kind of world we can enjoy living in all over the Earth.

"Flavr Savr"
June 26 & 27, 1992

Geri asked me what I thought of the new, genetically-altered tomato that was recently in the news. The federal government had just decided that genetically-engineered foods will require no special testing or regulation.

The ruling was inspired by the "Flavr Savr" tomato which may be on the market next year. This tomato's DNA has been altered so that it no longer produces the enzyme that causes the fruit to soften and rot. This means that the tomato can be grown in California or Mexico, for example, picked at red ripeness, shipped across the United States or the Pacific, handled at the wholesale and retail level, and still be edible. When you grow tomatoes in your garden, or get them from a farmer nearby, these new qualities are irrelevant. They are designed specifically for a food system with a great distance between the farm and the dinner table.

The recent decision dealt solely with food safety issues. The ruling basically said that the government will assume that genetically-altered food is safe unless the levels of naturally occurring toxins are increased, allergens are introduced or nutrient levels are significantly altered. So cucumbers with tuna protein, or potatoes with chicken genes are okay, because they are made of substances already found in foods. This ruling also probably means that, unless it is commercially valuable to let consumers know which foods are altered, such foods won't be labeled.

115

Remembering our experiences with lead in gasoline, pesticides like DDT and Agent Orange, and substances like chlorofluorocarbons, we have good reason to be suspicious now. Each of these had a profit-hungry corporate giant pushing the government to let it introduce its new technology. Our tax-supported government served the interests of corporations, rather than the safety of the public. At the time the lead additive to gasoline was approved, its opponents gave the same arguments that were eventually used to remove it 70 years later, after a lot of expensive research, regulation and health damage.

It's clear from reading the financial press that the goal of agricultural biotechnology is not to feed the starving people of the world, although that may be given as a justification. As reported in *Barrons*, the chairman of the company which developed the "Flavr Savr" tomato reckons that wholesale sales of fresh tomatoes are roughly $3.5 billion and are growing 10 percent a year. He says, "We think if we just look at the super-premium end of the market, we'll have a $150 million business in short order, and ultimately it could be a $500 million business." Wall Street responded to the government ruling with a 52-week high price for this tomato producer's stock.

Articles in the business pages trumpet that the "Flavr Savr" is just the beginning for an agricultural biotechnology industry whose investors are expecting big returns.

We may never know for sure about the safety of this tomato, or of the corn which produces an insecticide, or of the use of hormones in cows and pigs, but safety is an effective smoke screen which often disguises the real issues.

The effects of almost all of the energy, chemical and capital-intensive, high-tech agricultural advances of this century have been devastating:
• Smaller farmers all over the world have been driven off the land.
• Our food now travels an average of 1,300 miles.

116

- Seventy-six percent of our food dollar goes to buy packaging, processing, advertising, marketing and transportation.
- Both genetic diversity and the freshness of our food have decreased.
- A significant percentage of people in Third World countries, and in American cities and rural areas are hungry, while our taxes go to subsidize excess food production.

Like the health-care industry, which spends enormous sums on elaborate computerized record-keeping systems and very costly machines (when the real needs are for prenatal care, nutrition information and simple inoculations), the agricultural sector turns to new, expensive and questionable products in order to create profits, when there are more important issues upon which to focus.

The real question is why, in order to get tasty tomatoes, do we need to give money, tax breaks and regulatory services to rich investors and corporate scientists, when it is so easy, so much fun, and so educational to grow tomatoes in our own backyards?

Diet and Evolution
June 28 & 29, 1991

Except during the last few decades of the thousands of years of human existence, people have found the foods they needed in their local environment. People, plants and animals have co-evolved in complex, multifunctional ways.

It has been reported that the !Kung San, natives of the Kalahari Desert (one of the more barren places on Earth) spend about 4 hours per week to provide all their basic needs. The rest of their time is spent with family and friends.

The native peoples of the far north, the Inuit and the Saami, feed themselves and live interesting and challenging lives in a place where much of the year we would see nothing but ice.

The Earth provides, and it doesn't seem outrageous, at a time when even dogs have different foods for different ages and energy levels, that maybe the people who live much of the year at below freezing temperatures may eat different foods than people who live much of the time in an environment near body temperature.

In *The New York Times*, Jane Brody recently reported a very strong link between diet and health among the native people of the American Southwest. Until the 1940s, the Pima and Tohono O'odham Indians ate foods such as mesquite pods, tepary beans and prickly pear cactus that grew prolifically in their desert environment. Mesquite pods are traditionally ground into a flour which is very high in minerals, protein, and soluble fiber and because its sweetness comes from fructose, it can be processed in the body without the use of insulin.

This report indicates just how tightly coupled diet, health and the environment can be. Among these Indians, the last four decades have seen a decrease in the cultivation and use of their native foods, and an increase in the consumption of processed, sweetened and refined foods. For example, our government has provided lard, refined wheat flour, sugar, coffee and processed cereals, and the fast-food, convenience-store, American diet has become more available. The transition from native diets to imported and processed foods has resulted in an increase in the incidence of diabetes and obesity. As much as half the population now has diabetes, which used to be rare, and many of these formerly trim people tip the scales at over 200 or even 300 pounds.

Native foods are high in soluble fibers and contain amylose, a type of starch which is digested very slowly. These two characteristics work together to provide a stable blood-sugar level and slow down digestion, as well as allow one to feel satisfied for longer periods.

118

There is even a pronounced difference in some very similar foods. For example, the pinto beans that the government provides are much more rapidly digested than native tepary beans, and they also are lower in protein. Our sweet corn contains sugars and starches which are rapidly digested and cause a rise in blood-sugar levels. Native corn is digested much more slowly and has less sugar. The slow release of energy from the native diet complements the native life style and the availability of foods.

Similar connections between a change in diet and a decrease in health have been found among Australian Aborigines, Pacific Islanders, and other peoples. Some even suggest that many Americans would be less prone to heart disease, high blood pressure, diabetes and obesity if they ate more whole grains, fresh fruits and vegetables and fewer processed and refined foods—more like the way our great grandparents ate.

In this context, government surplus food gifts look like weapons, slowly but surely destroying their recipients. What does it mean for the health of this planet's citizens when American-based corporations sell the same foods and beverages to people all over the world? These foods and beverages come not from the slow evolution of diet, health and the environment, but from the fast-track evolution of profit and our lopsided economic system. This is a diet designed to produce money, not health.

With a garden, we eat very locally, and closer to the way the vast majority of our ancestors ate.

Freedom of Speech
July 5 & 6, 1991

There's an old saying that goes, "He who pays the piper, calls the tune."

Recently, a radio commentator used this saying to describe the Supreme Court's upholding of the executive branch's prohibition of the mention of abortion in federally-assisted clinics. More simply, it said that the executive branch of government could forbid discussion of a certain topic if some portion of the funding came from the government.

The First Amendment to the Constitution says, "Congress shall make no law respecting an establishment of religion, or prohibiting the free exercise thereof; or abridging the freedom of speech, or of the press, or the right of the people peaceably to assemble, and to petition the government for a redress of grievances."

We were well educated about the importance of this amendment in school, and it may even be a more universal human sentiment. We should regard all of these rights as nearly sacred.

As the daily war reports came in from the Persian Gulf, I remember being relieved when I heard that the environmental damage from the oil spill there was not as bad as some scientists had thought. My already eroded belief in the government crumbled weeks later when it was revealed that this statement was speech commanded and constrained by the executive branch.

The idea that "he who pays controls what can be said" is especially disturbing after a decade which has seen unprecedented concentration in the control of money and other resources in the federal government and the corporate world.

If our government is really "Of, by, and for the people," when we hear the word "government," we should hear "us."

The 1980s deregulation and tax cuts gave some of the

120

largest corporations a negative tax rate, i.e., they got credits or money back from the government. In many cases this allowed them to expand further into businesses which supply the government with weapons, computers and services, and to increase their global control of capitol, goods and information.

There was also concentration of power in the executive branch of government. And, as the federal government shed responsibilities (ranging from education and care of the needy, to responsible supervision in our behalf of banks, airlines, insurance companies, defense contractors and S&Ls), state and local governments were left with greatly increased responsibilities and less money.

These concentrations of power and wealth, and the distancing of most of us from the ability to affect the government, mirror the concentrations of and distancing from our food and energy sources.

The more we let large entities satisfy our needs for food, shelter and entertainment, the more subject we are to their control, and the more money they have to "pay the piper."

It seems that unless we work very hard, our First Amendment rights will disappear while we are distracted by our planet's diminishing ability to sustain life, as the powers-that-be struggle to promote the illusion that we can have it all. It may be that our current high-consumption, distant and energy-intensive life style implies limits to free speech.

As we celebrate our nation's freedom and the grand vision which inspired many of its founders, we realize that our basic rights are under attack. Only if we assume greater personal, family and community responsibility for all aspects of our lives, do we have any hope of regaining the control we have handed over to the government and corporations.

Eating from the Garden: Blackcaps
July 12 & 13, 1991

For several weeks now, we've been picking and eating blackcap raspberries. We have had raspberries crushed with maple syrup on toast, raspberries and maple syrup and cream for dessert and raspberries blended with other fruits in a drink. We have put away raspberry jam, raspberry/mango chutney and have some raspberry wine in the works. And almost every day, we eat fresh raspberries right from the canes as we go to the garden or solar shower.

Blackcaps, or black raspberries, *Rubus occidentalis* botanically, are native to North America. Their berries are a little smaller and firmer than the typical red raspberry. They grow wild almost anywhere there is a niche for them—some open ground in a shady place. One patch by the road has been producing with no care other than picking for over 12 years. The patch on the north side of my son Dan's room has been expanding slowly for years, with only minimal care. This involves the removal of shrubs or poison ivy vines which invade the patch and some pruning in the winter to shorten the canes and remove the ones which bore fruit last year. Raspberries have a 2-year cycle. They send up a cane the first year and produce fruit on laterals of that cane the second year. Some varieties of red raspberries complete both steps in one year, however.

Raspberries need plenty of organic matter as mulch on the soil around them. Their canes retain any leaves which fall into the vicinity, so the soil stays covered, which builds up fertility.

Blackcaps are recognizable most of the year by their gracefully arching canes with a slight purplish or whitish color. When the tips touch the ground, they often root. In this way, the patch expands. Of course they also spread when a bird eats some berries and then sits on a branch or fence post and defecates. The seed falls to the ground surrounded by nutrients.

It is interesting to think that blackcap patches have been tended, and these berries have been eaten by the people of this region for thousands of years. I'm sure the Native Americans knew where the best patches were and helped to maintain them.

Just now as the blackcap patches slow down in their production, the red and golden raspberries, dewberries and thimbleberries begin to bear well, and the blackberries swell.

All of these bramble fruits seem to do better if they are picked regularly. When the ripe berries aren't picked, they frequently get moldy and seem to discourage other berries on the same cane from ripening.

Raspberries provide a good example of the difference between eating from the garden and eating from the supermarket. The period of production of most fruits and vegetables makes for a short-term sameness in the diet with changes throughout the year, while the industrial food system produces a short-term variety with a long-term sameness.

Recently 2-year-old Stephanie Rose visited from Manhattan. Early on, Suzanne offered her a bowl of blackcaps. After polishing those off without hesitation, little Stephanie wanted to know where they came from. Once she learned, she spent the rest of the weekend taking the adults back to the patch to pick and eat with her.

Stephanie found out what the Native Americans knew, that with a little personal involvement and the natural productivity of the Earth, delicious food abounds. With an energy-intensive, distant food system, such delicious berries are rarely available, and only for a high price.

Soda Cans and Salmon
July 19 & 20, 1991

Before we can begin to solve any of our environmental problems, we have to realize how close we are, each of us, to the cause of the problem, and the complexity of the path which got us here.

In the case of the near extinction of several species of salmon in the Pacific Northwest, we literally hold one of the causes in our hands. It's that light-weight, quick-chilling, oh-so convenient and "recyclable" aluminum can. Americans use more aluminum beverage cans than the rest of the world combined. We comprise only about 5 percent of the Earth's population, yet we use over half of the aluminum beverage cans in the entire world.

Aluminum is a *very* energy-intensive material. It requires such an enormous quantity of electricity to smelt this ore that it has actually been called "congealed electricity." It requires more than 6 times the energy to produce an aluminum can than it does to make a steel can.

During the New Deal in the 1930s, dams on the Columbia River in Oregon and Washington were built with tax dollars to produce jobs, electricity, recreation and water for irrigation. With a large supply of low-cost, taxpayer-subsidized electricity, the aluminum smelters moved in. They currently pay about 40 percent less than the national average for electricity.

When many of us were youngsters, if we drank a soda, or our parents drank a beer, the chances were that it came in a glass bottle from a local bottler or brewery. The bottle had been used before to hold a beverage, and, after we were done, it would be returned, washed and refilled.

Then in the 1960s, the drink sellers discovered that they could market the container for a beverage as well as its contents. Remember all the advertising brainwash which told us how great "no deposit-no return" containers were? Between

1950 and 1967, while population rose 30 percent and beer consumption rose 37 percent, use of non-returnable beer bottles rose *595 percent*. Of course the ads didn't tell us that we would be responsible for disposal costs or about the overcrowded landfills this approach would eventually create. They also didn't mention the fact that once we didn't have to return the bottles anymore, the bottlers and brewers—much like the dairy farms with the advent of throw-away milk containers—could move out of our communities, to be concentrated in a few locations owned by just a few large corporations.

But back to the salmon. For thousands of years these special fish have used the great rivers of the Northwest for spawning, having evolved a complex and successful life cycle in the environment. Big dams make major changes in the environment. Managing a river's flow with big dams for maximum production of cheap electricity effects even greater change in the environment, often making rivers unusable by the salmon. With their life cycle interrupted, their population declines.

Without cheap electricity, aluminum would have been too expensive for single-use cans. If the full costs of the tax subsidies for the electricity, long-distance trucking and disposal, and a warning label about the extinction of several species of salmon and local varieties of beer and soda had been included with each aluminum can, we probably would have stayed with refillable, returnable bottles.

Big dams gave us big brewers and bottlers, big trash piles, and less diversity in the world.

Of course other uses of aluminum have also greatly expanded since the 1950s—siding, which is 150 times as energy-intensive as wood, cooking pots and pans, TV dinner trays (before the microwave made metal containers less useful) and aluminum foil. Our knowledge of aluminum has expanded, too. We've learned that acid precipitation makes it more available in the soil, and that this availability damages the forests in New England. We've also learned how acid foods release aluminum from cooking utensils, and the possible connection

125

between aluminum and Alzheimer's disease.

It's a complex web we have woven as a society. We cannot have it all. We can't have aluminum cans cheap enough to throw away and a sustained salmon population.

The health of the aluminum industry and the health of our planet may not be compatible.

Daylilies
July 24 & 25, 1992

One of the most distinctive features of our July landscape is the widespread presence of the beautiful red and orange daylilies now in bloom. From the enormous sweeps naturalized along country roads, to large clumps in carefully manicured gardens or a single plant enlivening a mail box, the common daylily runs like a golden thread through the Northeastern environment. In some Vermont towns, it seems that half the houses have a large stand of these daylilies in front of the bright white flowers of Annabelle hydrangeas. What a sight.

The daylily, whose botanical name *Hemerocallis* comes from the Greek meaning "beautiful for a day," is so ubiquitous, it is hard to believe that it is not native to this region. Daylilies are naturalized here, meaning that they grow and thrive without our care. Native to Eurasia, they spread westward through Europe and England and on into our region in colonial times.

Each spring, large clumps of 2-foot-long, grass-like leaves emerge quickly from the daylilies' tuberous roots. Stiff, leafless flower stalks grow up to 5 feet tall and bear 10 to 20 buds, which open, 1 or 2 at a time, each just for a day. A mature clump, which spreads from the roots, can have many

126

flower stalks, so there is quite a show. As they spread from the roots, they establish themselves into thick stands.

One of the reasons (aside from its beauty) that people have spread this plant around the world is that the tubers, sprouting stalks, buds and dried flowers are edible, and the root and crown have medicinal uses.

For centuries, the Chinese have gathered and dried the buds and flowers to give flavor and an okra-like gelatinous quality to soups and stews. Called "golden needles," they are common in hot and sour soup.

In his wonderful book, *Stalking the Wild Asparagus*, Euell Gibbons recommends preparing the unopened buds like green beans, boiling them for a few minutes and serving with butter. He also gives recipes for battered and fried buds, and for a stir-fry using them. He recommends preparing the one-half by one inch tubers by boiling in salted water. Although the tubers can be gathered anytime when the ground isn't frozen, at this time of year the young white tubers are the best. They have a delicious nutty flavor and can be eaten raw.

In the spring, the sprouting leaf stalks can be cut off just below the ground. With the outer leaves removed, they can be sliced into salads or cooked like asparagus.

Euell Gibbons' books are wonderful resources. They have provided me with inspiration and knowledge important for my appreciation of our region's plants.

Wyman's Gardening Encyclopedia also provides valuable information. Daylily flowers are a high-protein, non-fattening food which is rich in minerals and vitamins A and B. For thousands of years, people in Asia have used the root and crown of this plant as a diuretic, to reduce fever, to relieve pain, and to treat piles, jaundice, and breast tumors.

These recommendations are specific to the wild 'Tawny daylily'. There are many other species and varieties of daylilies, and breeders have made so many crosses that *Wyman's* lists over a hundred named varieties, with colors ranging from red and purple, to melon, light cream and yellow. One of my favorites is 'Hyperion,' an elegant and graceful plant with fragrant, clear yellow flowers. Daylilies are easily propagated by dividing the clumps.

The naturalized daylilies are at home in a variety of soils, in sun or part shade, and thrive without our care. What a sensible and beautiful way to get both nutrition and healing.

Fractal Beef
July 26 & 27, 1991

The notice on the food store bulletin board says, "Save the rain forest, become a vegetarian, today."

In their ads, the Beef Industry Council reminds us that beef fits into today's life styles.

Is there some middle ground?

The Gaia hypothesis postulates that the Earth, whose Goddess was called Gaia by the Greeks, behaves as if it is an organism, with living things and the environment evolving together, each affecting the other. James Lovelock, an originator of the Gaia hypothesis has written: "There can be no prescription, or set of rules for living within Gaia. For each of our different actions, there are only consequences."

For years we have been discovering more about the consequences of our current industrial approach to raising beef. Large concentrations of cattle in feedlots produce large concentrations of manure which find their way into the groundwater, and large quantities of methane which find their way into the atmosphere and increase the greenhouse effect.

These cattle in feedlots need mountains of grain to be fattened for market. The growing of this grain, which would produce much more human nutrition if fed to people directly (instead of being processed through cows), frequently depletes groundwater supplies and contaminates the land with fertilizers and pesticides. Before they are sent to the feedlot, many of the cattle have roamed the public range-lands of the West in concentrations great enough to do serious harm to vegetation and streams. And, indeed, much of the rain forest in some Central and South American countries has been cleared to provide pasture for cattle to feed North Americans. This is pasture which is not sustainable in that region.

We also have discovered that fat concentrates in the bodies of people who eat a lot of meat and that control of the beef industry is now concentrated in the hands of a few very large corporations.

Yet, animals play an important role in the ecosystem and for most of human history, they have played a part in the our diet.

The deep fertility of our country's Great Plains evolved from the symbiotic relationship between the bison, which roamed the prairie in massive numbers for centuries until they were nearly wiped out by white men, and the grasses which grew there. Like cows, bison are ruminants. They can digest grasses (which we can't) and turn them into useful food. On my farm, over the dozen or so years that I had a few cows on the land, I could see the improved fertility as they were moved around to graze. Their manure and urine enriched the soil, encouraged more useful kinds of plants and made the grass grow better.

One of the more interesting and useful concepts for understanding the world is the notion of fractals, or fractal geometry. This theory says, in part, that a pattern remains the same at different scales. For example, the smallest capillaries in our circulatory systems have the same design as our largest veins. The pattern is scale-invariant. In fractal terms, the microscopic capillaries are symmetrical with the veins; without a scale reference, we couldn't tell which we were looking at.

The beef industry also illustrates this notion of fractal symmetry. The pattern in this industry is to ignore the relationship of animals and the environment and to encourage excessive concentration on the land, in corporate structures and in our bodies.

Just as a moderate amount of beef in a diet that also includes grains, fresh fruits and vegetables combined with a life style that includes regular exercise and other good habits, can be useful nutritionally, the proper ratio of cows to land can benefit both the cows and the land. And just as a given amount of beef will have a different effect on an athletic teenager and a sedentary middle-aged smoker, for example, a given number of cows will have different effects on 40 acres of good Vermont farmland and 40 acres of dry western rangeland or cleared rain forest.

As Lovelock says, "There can be no prescription, or set of rules for living within Gaia. For each of our different actions, there are only consequences."

One serious consequence of our distant, industrial food system is that fewer of us have enough direct experience and knowledge of Gaia to find the appropriate middle ground between becoming a vegetarian and eating more beef.

Early August Planting
August 2 & 3, 1991

We are not yet halfway from the solstice to the equinox; 7 weeks of summer are left, and there is plenty of time to grow some vegetables for good fresh eating this fall.

Last year on the first of August, we planted 2 types of edible-podded peas and 2 kinds of bush beans, plus radishes and beets. We started harvesting the beans on October 2 and picked them for 3 weeks. The peas, which are more at home in cool weather, produced a little longer.

Depending on variety, beans and peas need 6 to 8 weeks to go through their cycle of growth, flowering and pod development. Our favorite of the late beans last year was the French horticultural bean, 'Triumph de Farcy,' which begins to bear in 48 days (a little longer in the waning day length of late summer) and with regular picking will produce until it is killed by a frost. Recently, Judy showed me the 10-foot row she had planted in 2 stages that produced many more beans than her family could possibly eat.

Other vegetables that are planted now will be ready to eat much sooner because the young plants can be used as they are thinned to make room for the remaining ones. Lettuce, carrots, beets, radishes and greens like mustard, spinach, kale, turnip, and arugula all take less than 60 days to grow and are not bothered by the first frosts. In fact, spinach, mustard and arugula take only 40 days to mature and will provide food for weeks after that. All these do well in the cooler weather and may even taste better after a frost.

One difficulty with August planting is getting the seeds to sprout. Germination for many plants increases with soil temperature up to 77 or 80 degrees Fahrenheit, but above that drops off rather quickly. If there is enough moisture to allow the seed to swell and split open as the radicle (embryonic root) emerges, but not enough to keep the young root moist, the plant may die. Careful attention to moisture levels is important. For spinach, chard and beets (which are all related) and for lettuce and carrots, Rodale Press's useful book, *How to Grow Vegetables and Fruits by the Organic Method*, recommends the following practice: Spread the seeds between two sheets of wet blotting paper and place in the refrigerator until they sprout. Then carefully sow the sprouted seeds and keep them moist until they are well-established. The standard planting depth is twice the thickness of the seed. In summer plantings, a greater depth may be useful, and you might thoroughly wet the row before planting.

As we move toward autumn, several factors slow the garden's growth; shorter days and lower temperatures mean that plants grow more slowly, and at some time in the next 2 to 4 months, a frost will injure or kill plants which are sensitive, e.g., beans, tomatoes, peppers, squash, marigolds and basil. The first frost is extremely variable. Last year our lower field was frosted in mid-September, more than a month before the garden behind the house. There is even greater variability, for example, between the hills of Litchfield, and the backyard gardens of Bridgeport, where the first frost may not come until December. When you plant at this time of year, plan to take advantage of the effects of microclimates. Sloping ground, the south side of a building (especially with a heat-storing foundation) or taller plants or trees nearby can all postpone the killing effects of early frosts.

It doesn't take much room for these fall vegetables. A small 4-foot square area planted with a mixture of greens will provide nutritious and tasty food well into November. It is worth planting now.

The Garbologist
August 7 & 8, 1992

R ecently there's been a lot of media coverage about the work of the Arizona garbologist. For years he has used archeologists' techniques to investigate our landfills. His data at first seem surprising, but given an understanding of landfills, they make sense. However, none of the reports I've listened to have drawn useful conclusions, and the data could easily lead people to actually draw erroneous conclusions.

This researcher found that paper comprises the largest percentage of a landfill's contents. Construction debris like wood, sheetrock and steel reinforcing bars are the second most plentiful. He found that plastic takes up a very small percentage of landfill space, and that materials we think of as biodegradable (like newspapers and hot dogs) don't decay much in a landfill. If we accept mixed waste landfills as a reasonable solution, this could lead us to the conclusion that paper and construction materials are problems in our society and plastics are not.

Paper, food wastes and non-treated wood are all biodegradable. In the presence of water, air and the living decomposers (i.e., molds, bacteria and fungi) they will become humus, the basis of fertile soil. These wastes which become useful in a matter of months through composting, are entombed for decades in a well-managed landfill because water and air are excluded. Only if there is a plastic coating on the paper, or if it is printed with toxic or heavy metal inks will the humus be unfit for growing food or flowers. Of course, much of the paper waste can be recycled into more paper, and waste wood may be useful for building houses or creating heat.

Landfills are a problem because they take up valuable acreage along our roads and our beautiful rivers and shoreline, and because they leak fluid leachate into surface and groundwater. The weight of the garbage, and of the dirt which is used to cover and seal the landfill acts like a giant press, squeezing out a frequently toxic mixture of juices.

Glass, steel and rocks or bricks just take up room. Their presence in a landfill is not much different from the ore deposits from which they came.

It is toxic materials like pesticides, solvents, heavy metal inks, and wood preservatives, and potentially dangerous materials like animal wastes and human wastes in disposable diapers which present the greatest danger from the leachate. Even though they are present in small quantities, they can pollute a large quantity of garbage. Some of these are the very materials which also render the ashes from a waste-to-energy plant dangerous.

And plastic: it doesn't decompose; it disappears only when burned. Of course, if carefully separated by number, it can be recycled into more plastic. But this scenario implies that the world will become increasingly filled with plastic. The more plastic we manufacture, the more of it will inevitably end up in the garbage. Its percentage will rise as other materials are recycled or composted. Plastic is likely to be a problem that sticks around for a long time.

The general lessons here: We should create systems that allow organic matter to decompose; we need to separate materials to recycle them; even small percentages of toxic materials can create lots of contamination when mixed with other wastes.

Reduce, reuse, recycle, compost: this is the garbage hierarchy. Reduce the amount of disposable things in our lives. Reuse everything we can. Recycle what we can't reuse, and compost all the organic matter that's left.

We've just started down this new road, and already Connecticut's waste-to-energy plant operators are saying that they don't have enough garbage to burn.

We allowed state and local governments and corporations to use public bond money to build excess garbage-burning capacity. Garbage is expensive, not only in its environmental effects and tax-paid disposal costs, but also in the energy, material and regulatory subsidies our federal taxes provide to producers of throw-away products.

Imagine a future where we all will spend less time taking out the trash.

Oil Junkies
August 9 & 10, 1991

I was reading Senator Lieberman's explanation of his opposition to one of the key provisions of President Bush's energy plan—drilling for oil in the Arctic National Wildlife Refuge. He quotes the Department of the Interior's description of this very special refuge as "the only conservation-system unit which protects in an undisturbed condition, a complete spectrum of the Arctic ecosystems in North America." The Senator notes that the most optimistic estimate of the total amount of oil in the refuge is equal to 200 days' worth of oil for our country. If oil companies can locate, produce and sell the oil buried below the fragile tundra, it would keep the U. S. from running out of oil for just over half of a year.

As I read this, the image of a drug addict came to mind. We've all heard about people who are so addicted to heroin or some other drug that they risk jail to break in and steal a very expensive stereo, for example, and then pawn it for just $50 to buy their next fix.

The psychiatric criteria for substance addiction, as reported in the July 13th *Science News* include the following symptoms:
- more use of the substance than intended.
- an unachieved desire to control or cut down on substance-use.
- continued use of the substance despite awareness of the problems it causes.
- a disproportionate amount of time spent on substance-related activities.
- a marked tolerance of and need for larger doses.
- replacement of normal daily activities by substance use.

We as a nation, and especially our current leaders, are oil junkies. The very thought that we would bring all the ugly, polluting, dangerous mess of the oil field to one of the last

135

great wildernesses on Earth for such a small return demonstrates our addiction.

The almost daily oil spills, the oil war, fires and politics of the Middle East, the increasing greenhouse effect, obscene profits of the oil companies, and dangerous air pollution ought to be enough to get us to stop. But no, the President says drill more so we won't be dependent on foreign oil.

Despite the fact that we use more energy per capita and unit of GNP than almost any other nation on Earth, the President says drill for more oil, develop new technologies to get additional oil out of existing wells and deregulate other aspects of the oil industry. And while we're at it, let's build lots of new nuclear power plants and develop other fuels.

We've known for at least several decades that conservation produces energy services more cheaply and cleanly than oil; yet this administration continues to resist new efficiency standards for cars.

Science News reports that the oil industry expects to spend $1.7 billion annually to develop the fields on the North Slope. This money will be spent in an attempt to simultaneously find oil deep below the surface and protect these delicate ecosystems from the roads, airstrips, pipelines and vast quantities of toxic wastes which result from the search for and production of oil. And if they find what they are looking for, they will sell it to us so we can burn it up, further fouling our air.

Imagine if we spent $1.7 billion annually on conservation measures. We would create jobs where people live, and the result of that spending, a lower demand for energy, would mean smaller energy bills and a cleaner environment. The Arctic National Wildlife Refuge belongs to all of us. We can spend enormous resources to despoil it and enrich the already wealthy, or we can put our resources where we are, and spread the value of conservation around.

If we cure our oil habit, we can spend less time on the highways and in our cars, and more time at those activities which were normal for people before the oil age: walking, gardening and enjoying the company of friends and family in a clean environment.

Sunday Dinner
August 14 & 15, 1992

One of the things Suzanne and I are trying to do is to discover how to feed ourselves.

We know it doesn't make sense to base our diet on food that's shipped from Mexico, Chile or even California. And there are too many news stories about the hazards of large-scale chicken farming (ranging from packing plant disasters, to water pollution and disease contamination) to feel good about buying the foam-and-plastic-wrapped chicken of commerce. We're not interested in spending the national average of 76¢ of each food dollar on transportation, packaging, advertising and retailing activities which consume energy, produce wastes, and frequently remove flavor, nutrition and freshness.

We had a meal the other night which made me think we might be closing in on it.

It was a Sunday evening after a gorgeous August day. Earlier, Danica and her family had brought to our farm the 3 one-month-old ducklings she hatched out, inspired by her high school ecology course. We spent a lot of time watching those cute little ducks.

The dinner was simple enough, All-American really. Thirteen-year-old Jon who was visiting has the food biases common to many youngsters. He doesn't like chunky tomatoes in his sauce, or cheese unless it is melted. Suzanne prepared baked chicken legs and thighs, steamed broccoli, marinated cucumber salad, and boiled new potatoes topped with a stir-fry of celery, garlic, shallots, and hot peppers.

We realized near the end of the meal that the only ingredients that we hadn't had a hand in producing were butter for the broccoli, olive oil for the stir-fry, vinegar and black and hot red peppers. We grew enough hot peppers last year to still have some, but we let them get frozen before they were dry. We won't make that mistake again.

Our friend Gary grew the chicken on his homestead in Litchfield County. We had traded him half of one of our pigs for some of his chickens and a turkey. About 2 weeks earlier, Suzanne and I spent a pleasant Saturday morning under a maple tree at Gary's house, turning 20 Cornish-Cross chickens he had raised for 6 or 7 weeks into packages of chicken for the freezer. Gary's had a tough time with coyotes in the last year. They like chicken too.

Gary's 8-year-old daughter expressed a culturally-correct horror at the proceedings, but admitted that she liked to eat chicken. Most of us have a grandmother or great-grandmother who thought nothing of going to the chicken house as the first step in preparing Sunday dinner. The taste of really fresh chicken, especially when the birds have eaten a wide variety of foods and had access to plentiful fresh air and sunshine, is hard to beat.

For our dinner, the chicken was simply baked with Hungarian paprika and fresh ground peppercorns. Its juices, skimmed of the fat, made the most delicious gravy. The Red Norland potato harvest was in. I put about 15 small potatoes in the ground in May, and that afternoon Jon and I dug up a half bushel ranging in size from 1 to 3 inches. Suzanne stir-fried some just-harvested celery, garlic and shallots with hot peppers as a topping for the potatoes. This celery is not the bland, blanched stuff from the store. It has thin, dark green stalks which are harvested a few at a time. Celery has recently been found to have a relaxing effect on the smooth muscle of the heart, a benefit to those with high blood pressure.

We find that using garlic and/or shallots in our cooking

138

eliminates the need for salt. It doesn't take much garden space to grow a nice supply of these valuable bulbs. In July and August, it's possible to harvest a lot of flavor from a very small area.

For salads, we've been marinating our plentiful cucumbers with vinegar, garlic, fresh onions, dill seeds, and peppercorns. Even though we make a big bowlful every day, they frequently are eaten before the full flavor is developed. It's a snack kids love and parents can feel good about.

Although we had put the large broccoli heads in the freezer, the plants still produced enough side shoots for our dinner.

Suzanne and I drank some homemade dandelion wine, and Jon had iced herb tea.

What a meal! Simple, elegant and home-grown.

FREE Food
August 16 & 17, 1991

They appeared in our mailboxes the same week — unsolicited, brightly-colored advertising flyers with the word FREE in bold black, bright red and yellow inks, repeated over and over again.

From the supermarket chain: "Buy one, get one... FREE." Ham, bacon, ice cream, mushrooms, frozen entrees and more, all the products of our industrial food system: "Buy one, get one... FREE."

The other flyer from a fast food chain trumpets "FREE PIZZA"; the small print says, "Buy one pizza and get a second one FREE, " in different combinations spread over the following 3 weeks.

It has been estimated that nearly one fifth of the world's

population doesn't get enough food to eat. That's almost a billion people scattered over the Earth in such countries as Brazil, the Soviet Union, the Philippines, Albania, India, Mexico, Ethiopia and the United States—nearly a billion people who can't get enough food energy to satisfy their daily requirements.

How is it then that these giants of our industrial food distribution system give away food in communities where there are very few hungry humans? Is this food really FREE?

I suggest that this FREE food is some of the most expensive food humans have ever eaten. They are able to advertise it as FREE because most of the direct and indirect costs of this food are paid for with our taxes, by our environment, and with the disintegration of our social system.

The basic equation of human food supply for thousands of years included the soil, water and sunlight, plants and animals, and human energy. Out of this equation came civilization and culture.

With the advent of the oil age, and the industrialization of agriculture and our food supply, the equation changed. Our taxes subsidized oil and nuclear energy production, so the more of this energy a business could put into its food products, the greater the possibilities for reaping the benefits of government subsidies.

Our taxes were used to encourage farmers to get bigger and to buy all the latest pesticides, farm machinery and energy-intensive fertilizers. The pizza flour or pork produced on these giant industrial farms seems cheap because the costs of eroded topsoil, polluted wells, and depleted aquifers are not included. Whether spilled into drinking water, spread on the land or stored as toxic waste, the enormous quantities of pesticides produced in our country cost the environment and taxpayers plenty. Our children's children will be paying for all this long after we've had our FREE pizza.

Tax dollars have paid for waste disposal, so it made sense to sell as much packaging as possible—another way of milking the system. Even the advertising flyers are paid for by us.

140

As advertising they are a tax-deductible business expense, and their heavy metal red and yellow inks will contaminate landfills or incinerator ash for years to come.

The greatest hidden costs of this food system are probably human. Before the advent of the oil age, the vast majority of people were directly connected with the productive fecundity of the Earth in a holistic way. They experienced daily the awe-inspiring wonder of the natural world. Now, the closest many of us get to the source of our food is advertising flyers, supermarkets and restaurants. And the largely hidden tragedy involves the legions of very low-paid American minorities and Third World brothers and sisters who labor under poor conditions on the industrial food system, cutting up pigs and chickens, cutting sugarcane and picking vegetables.

By giving us this exorbitantly expensive, so-called FREE food, the industrial food system is trying to deepen our dependence on the high energy-use, pollution and human exploitation it depends upon. If we forget how to grow our own food, they will have attained their goal of complete control.

The Morning After
August 20 & 21, 1993

It was the morning after a wonderful 25th wedding anniversary party.

Harvey, the groom's brother, a former hospital administrator, now a consultant in his 50s, Trudy, the bride's aunt, a biochemist in her 70s, retired from the National Institutes of Health, my wife, Suzanne, the bride's college roommate, a teacher in her 40s, and myself were visiting in the happy couple's home before brunch. The smell of coffee turned the conversation to caffeine. Harvey told us about a pain he had had in his stomach. It was thought to be an ulcer. One simple test revealed nothing. A fancier test was done, still nothing. Finally, an expensive and very uncomfortable test was undertaken. Nothing showed up, except a bill for over $1,000.

Someone suggested that he stop drinking coffee because of the caffeine. So he did, and the pain stopped. Since then he has used only decaffeinated coffee, and the pain has stayed away.

Trudy reported she had experienced persistent diarrhea, which doctors couldn't get rid of. She stopped drinking caffeinated beverages and eating wheat, and her trouble ended.

Suzanne reported her experience with painful fibrocystic tissue in her breasts for 15 years, especially around the time of her menstrual period. On the advice of friends, she stopped using caffeine and her pain went away.

I didn't remember it at the time, but as I thought about this piece, I realized that I had stopped drinking coffee after I began to be bothered with a dull pain in my neck each morning after drinking coffee. I switched to organic green tea, in part because of the ecological and social disasters coffee growing produces in Third World countries. Pesticides used on coffee contaminate large areas of the tropics, and women and children work for very low wages picking coffee beans for large, wealthy landowners.

However, one particularly early and busy morning I had a second cup of the green tea, which contains some caffeine, and the pain in my neck returned for several hours.

None of the information in this true story is approved by the American medical establishment, or, of course, by the purveyors of caffeine.

Back at the brunch table, while drinking herbal tea, we were sharing this health information with others at the party. Some of the guests didn't know that chocolate also contains caffeine. Most knew that many cola drinks contain significant amounts of caffeine. I didn't realize until researching this piece that a dose of some over-the-counter painkillers contains as much caffeine as a cup of coffee.

I looked up caffeine in *The Wellness Encyclopedia* from the University of California. It notes that caffeine is a mildly habit-forming, mind-altering drug, yet puts most reports of caffeine's negative health effects in the category of myth. Under benign breast disease, it says that a study of 3,300 women by the National Institutes of Health found no relationship between caffeine consumption and fibrocystic disease. It notes that, "Nor is there any evidence that giving up caffeine by itself eases the discomfort some women experience."

The bottom line here is about the discrepancy between the results of medical science and the knowledge gained from personal experience. It doesn't matter if 3,300 women aren't helped by quitting caffeine; if Suzanne is—and I've witnessed the benefits—it makes sense for her to stop.

We need to pay at least as much attention to our bodies and to the experiences of our friends, as we do to the medical establishment. Where caffeine is concerned, it can help us avoid a pain in the neck, breasts, stomach or rear end.

What are People Going to Do?
August 30 & 31, 1991

As we look toward the future, we might ponder the question: "What are people going to do?"

As giant banks merge to form megabanks so they can lay off people and save money, and defense contractors announce market-rallying layoffs to cut costs, we wonder: "What are people going to do?"

In a recent radio interview, an African-American father from Ohio said he wanted his daughter to go to college so she could meet the needs of "the technology of the future." Are we going to put the needs of technology ahead of the needs of people?

Already, robots build our cars and computers trade stocks and call us on the phone. What are people going to do?

The Wall Street investment banker said on the radio that there will be large-scale unemployment in East Germany as the industries there absorb a lot of capital to make factories more efficient. With more efficient factories, fewer people will be needed to turn out the products which, after a more or less brief use, will be outmoded and thrown away.

The investment bankers hope to convince us that efficient production in expensive factories is an important goal. This will make the resource they control, i.e., money, more valuable.

The European countries fear a massive influx of refugees from the former Soviet Union who are looking for work. What are people going to do?

We humans have evolved a wonderful set of skills through our long history. Our combination of mental capacity, manual dexterity, sensual acuity and emotional richness is remarkable and probably unequaled in any other species. Our bodies and our minds serve us best when they get regular exercise. Aside from artists and athletes, not many jobs make use of the whole range of human skills.

Let's get specific. Except in a modern technological society, people feed themselves by hunting, gathering and growing their food; clothe themselves by making, sewing and knitting garments; shelter themselves by building housing from local materials; and educate their children by involving them in these essential activities. All of this work makes good use of our minds, bodies and senses. The use of some technology, a good hoe, knitting needles, a sewing machine, an electric saw or a certain level of specialization can ease this work without changing its nature.

In our society, however, and especially in the future envisioned by international bankers and corporate planners, all of these holistic activities are removed from us and given to specialized machines, factories, agribusinesses and entertainment facilities which consume energy and other resources, and turn out mass-produced housing, clothing, food and fun. This approach needs two kinds of workers: a few highly-trained and specialized people to design, operate and repair machines, and a mass of people who are poorly paid to perform those activities which machines can't do yet. Frequently, as with computer-connected phone operators and assembly line workers, the pace and nature of this work is controlled by the machine. And many more people who are made useless by the barrage of mass-produced goods must either find employment in the service sector or remain unemployed. These cheap goods, so valued by our economic system, devalue the work of individuals. With eggs from the factory farm selling for 69¢ a dozen, the work to care for a small home flock of chickens has almost zero money value.

Personal experience often shows that without some meaningful, productive work, an individual's sense of self-worth declines. The more holistic and varied a work experience is, the more likely that it also will be satisfying.

What needs should we meet—the needs of technology to become more advanced, the needs of the capitalists to invest large sums of money, or the needs of people to have useful, productive work?

This Labor Day, let's put the needs of people first. Human-scale production creates quality and satisfaction that machines can't.

What are people going to do?

Global Work
September 4 & 5, 1992

I t's Labor Day weekend. Let's talk about work. Paul lives in Texas and was employed by the phone company. He started there after military service and rose to the role of manager in fiber-optic construction. Now in his 40s, and near the peak of his skills and earning potential, he has been forced into early retirement, just before his twin daughters head off to college.

Charline from Connecticut has a Bachelor's degree in marketing and just earned a Master's degree in education. She wants to teach, but is unable to find a job.

In the United States, millions of people have been laid off, and hundreds of thousands of young people, if they can find work, are laboring for minimum wage in order to distribute the plentiful goods from giant international corporations' tax-subsidized production, e.g. fast food, gasoline, CDs, electronics and clothes.

Millions more are working at jobs producing pesticides, enormous earthmoving equipment, weapons or TV shows that the world would be better off without. These jobs depend on our tax dollars, or produce environmental or social degradation, or they do all three.

Currently, local governments and utility companies give tax breaks, lower rates and sweetheart deals to businesses to get them to continue providing jobs in our communities.

If we live (as we are ever more frequently told) in a global economy, we should consider some little talked about aspects of global work.

Several weeks ago, Miquel told me about his friend Juanita who picks coffee beans for a wealthy landowner in Guatemala. Working diligently for 10 hours, she can pick 100 pounds of beans. For this she earns $1—about 10¢ an hour—or 1¢ per pound of coffee.

146

Juanita's children also pick coffee. Together, the 3 of them can pick 100 pounds in a 10-hour day. The dollar that they earn is essential to their family's survival, so they pick coffee instead of going to school. Their father was killed by the Guatemalan military, which probably used weapons and training provided by our tax dollars. His death might have occurred because he was working to change the system in his country where 5 percent of the people own 80 percent of the land, and children work for 30¢ a day instead of going to school.

Harper's magazine reports that in the country of Indonesia, Sadisah makes athletic shoes to be sold by the "Just Do It" company, earning $1.50 for a 10.5 hour day. Because it takes just 50 minutes of work to make a pair of shoes, the labor cost for these $80 shoes is just 12¢. Over 80 percent of the workers in Sadisah's factory are women and the majority of them are malnourished. A typical rental shanty has no running water or electricity.

It is important to realize that if Juanita and her children were paid 40 times as much, it would add a mere 1¢ to our cost for a cup of coffee.

It Sadisah were paid 20 times what she currently makes per hour, only $2.50 would be added to the price of a pair of those $80-sneakers.

A recent news report said that those American icons, GI Joe and Barbie dolls are now made by children laboring in China.

Other reports tell of our tax dollars being given to large drug companies to create jobs in Puerto Rico.

Millions of our brothers and sisters of color are jammed into small areas without jobs, trees, grass, or hope, while their countrymen enjoy golf courses and American style malls. This description from South Africa also fits much of urban America.

These examples just begin to scratch the surface of the injustices implicit in global work.

The North American Free Trade Agreement (Nafta) will allow United States corn (cheap because of energy, tax and environmental subsidies) into Mexico, which could drive over one million Mexican farmers off the land and into cities. Nafta will also allow inexpensively produced Mexican glass into our country, putting workers in small town glass factories in the United States out of work.

All over the Earth, there is a pressing need for the basics: safe drinking water, adequate and nutritious food, affordable housing, education and ecological waste disposal. Even though in most cases these needs are more easily met in the countryside, concentrated control of land and the resources of production and cheap food have been used worldwide to drive people off the land (and out of a sufficient and productive life style) into the cities and dependency.

Our work should be clear: providing the basics for everyone on Earth, and striving for peace. Global understanding may be more important than global trade in planning a future where we all have adequate, satisfying and productive work.

Freedom, Democracy and the Global Market Economy
September 6 & 7, 1991

S everal months ago, in explaining our government's attitude toward the changes that were occurring in the Soviet Union, a radio commentator mentioned that the Bush administration supports a united Soviet Union because it better serves American commercial interests.

Recently, a radio reporter described one of the elaborate facilities which belonged to the now defunct Communist Party in the USSR, with imported furniture, fancy dining facilities, art collections, exercise rooms, and limousines. It sounded much like the offices of a major corporation anywhere in the world.

The chairman of Philip Morris Companies Inc., the world's largest tobacco company which also sells a lot of beer and processed food products, is quoted in an Associated Press article about the move by some universities to withdraw their investments from tobacco companies. He says, "Investment decisions by fiduciaries should reflect the judgment of a prudent investor and should not be based on issues of social policy." He is saying that financial matters can and should be separated from social issues.

Freedom and democracy, and the global market economy seem to be the buzzwords of this administration. It envisions a future with countries called democracies in which daily life is dominated by giant global corporations.

Whose freedom are we talking about? And, where's the democracy?

President Bush's foreign policy seems to be based on making the world safe for multinational corporations. The negotiations for GATT and Nafta, most favored nation status for China, Middle East arms sales, and relations with former communist nations are all designed to increase the freedom and success of giant American corporations.

Before we allow ourselves to be further bulldozed into the global market economy, we need to realize the difference between money and value. To many human beings, the most valuable things cannot be reduced to the simple money numbers which the market requires. The old song says, "The best things in life are free." I suggest that they are also priceless— love, helping and watching children learn and grow up, peace, the wonders of the natural world, true freedom, and the inspiration of noble acts.

These important and wonderful things, which are outside the money economy, will suffer if the world is increasingly dominated by those whose vision (like that of the chairman of Philip Morris) is narrowed to money as the abstract judge of our actions.

Freedom is very important to the giant global industrial, financial, and service corporations. They want the freedom to enter every market, the freedom to move their goods around with a minimum of taxes, the freedom to move their factories to whichever country currently has the most attractive mix of low wages, tax benefits, subsidies, and minimum regulation of environmental and safety issues. In return, nearly everyone in the world will get the freedom, if they have the money, to choose whether to drink "The Right One Baby" or "The Real Thing"; whether their burger is charbroiled or fried; or which luxury sedan to buy, in a choice that mirrors our choice of which 'Republicrat' we want to occupy the White House. In reality, there's little or no difference between the options.

And democracy is not so important to multinational corporations. They have done very well in countries with dictators like Pinochet, Marcos, and Samoza, and in places like South Africa and Kuwait. This is not surprising, as they are run by interlocking boards of directors whose only loyalty is to increasing the return on investment to the shareholders, including themselves.

The really important decisions are outside the scope of most democracies. We need the right to choose between the high energy, global corporate economy which makes everyone dependent on distant sources, and a local economy which everywhere meets the real needs of people—to choose between a culture created by advertising for the financial enrichment of corporations, or a culture which respects and learns from the wisdom of native people the world over.

Garlic

September 11 & 12, 1992

Of all the vegetables we grow, Suzanne is proudest of the garlic. This year (just the second we've grown it) 50 pounds of garlic bulbs were harvested from about 100 feet of row.

Each clove we put in the ground last fall produced a whole bulb by late July. Most are good-sized, many close to 3 inches in diameter with 7 to 10 big cloves inside a sturdy, but easy-to-peel skin. We grow garlic because it tastes so good. It adds such wonderful flavor and aroma to foods ranging from fresh garden salsa and coleslaw, to stir-fried greens and omelets, not to mention that late summer classic, pesto.

There are two things you need to know in order to grow great garlic: when to plant and what to plant. Garlic is best planted between mid-October and mid-November—early enough so that it develops a good root system before the winter freeze, but not so soon that it sends up leaves which would be injured in the winter. For best results, you should plant garlic which was grown in this region, and is adapted to our climate. Most of the garlic sold in stores is grown in coastal California and will not do well here.

Garlic thrives using standard organic growing techniques. It needs a deeply-dug soil that is rich in organic matter. Suzanne used composted chicken manure. This not only provides the nutrients needed by garlic, but also will hold enough water so that the bulbs will fill out nicely the following summer. Individual cloves are planted, root end down, the top about 1 inch below the ground, each 4 to 6 inches from its neighbors in a row, or in a 1.5-to-4-foot wide bed.

Soon after it's planted, the row or bed should be mulched. We use hay or straw, but David and Kathleen in Thomaston use 2 inches of well-composted cow manure over the winter and add 2 inches of chopped leaves in the spring after the garlic leaves are 3 to 4 inches high. Ron, who wrote

151

Growing Great Garlic, prefers to use fresh clippings from tall grass.

The mulch will keep the ground warm in the fall which allows the roots to develop. Mulch also helps to keep the ground frozen once it freezes, so the developing bulbs don't get pushed out of the ground by alternate freezing and thawing during the winter.

If the mulch is loose enough for the garlic to push through in the spring, it can be left on to discourage weed growth. It is very important to control weeds in May and June, because this is when the plants need to put on enough growth to be able to fill out their bulbs as they start to swell after the solstice.

The two main types of garlic are softneck and hardneck (or top set). Most growers in this region grow the hardneck variety, but Julie in Barre, Massachusetts grows the softneck so she can braid it for sale. The softneck is the type most often sold in stores. It has a greater number of smaller cloves than the hard neck. The hardneck type sends up a flower stalk (or scape) in early summer which should be cut off to encourage maximum bulb size. These scapes are delicious.

Humans have eaten garlic for at least 10,000 years. Five thousand years ago in Sumeria, the first prescription for garlic was chiseled into a clay tablet. A shortage of garlic to feed the slaves building the pyramids in ancient Egypt caused the first recorded labor strike. Indian, Greek and Roman physicians recommended garlic for many health problems, and it was widely used in the Middle Ages as a multipurpose preventative medicine and cure-all. In World War I, infected battle wounds were treated with fresh garlic juice. In World War II, it was used successfully when Russia's supply of penicillin ran out.

It shouldn't be surprising that what people have discovered through direct experience over the course of 5,000 years has some basis which is provable by modern science. Recent studies have found that garlic has broad-spectrum antibiotic properties which kill tuberculosis and food-poisoning bacteria. It also has some anti-fungal properties.

Research has shown that garlic does at least three things which are good for your heart: It reduces blood pressure, decreases cholesterol and prevents harmful clots. Other studies show that garlic has promise for reducing blood sugar levels in diabetics, reducing the risk of cancer, eliminating lead from the body, treating leprosy and increasing immune function in AIDS patients.

For many of these healing effects, the garlic must be crushed so that its alliin and an enzyme come together to produce the antibiotic allicin. Because of the delicacy of this reaction (so easily started with the side of a knife in your kitchen) many commercial garlic preparations may not be effective. This is okay with us, because fresh from our garden, garlic is so flavorful and delicious.

Try growing some yourself.

September Garden Report
September 13 & 14, 1991

N ow, in mid-September, the garden is overflowing with food.

Turn your back for a few minutes and there's another basket of ripe tomatoes which need to be picked, more cucumbers, and of course zucchini and summer squash ready to grow to baseball-bat-size if not picked.

The equinox and the full Harvest Moon are a week from Monday. We are aware of how quickly the days are getting shorter. From the beginning to the end of June or December, there is only 11 minutes difference in day length. In contrast, the sun is up on the first of September for 82 minutes longer than on the 30th. In addition, as the Earth's tilt takes the sun below the equator, the time of twilight becomes shorter.

It seems as if the peppers, as well as the tomatoes and cucurbits (i.e. plants in the gourd family) sense this change and realize they have to ripen their seed-bearing fruits in abundance to assure the existence of their progeny. The ripening of the peppers is especially welcome. Their flavor is so much better (and sometimes hotter) when they are ripe and red.

The turnip and mustard greens planted on August 2 are now producing well. With ruby red and green chard, arugula and broccoli side shoots, they provide the basis for many of our dinners. They are stir-fried in olive oil flavored with recently harvested garlic and shallots, several types of peppers and fresh basil and parsley. Served over pasta, topped with chopped tomatoes, freshly grated parmesan and ground black pepper, a meal which always satisfies hunger and pleases the palate is the result. The exact mixture of ingredients varies, but the wonderful taste of our garden food makes eating almost anywhere else somewhat disappointing.

Like the plant's rush to reproduce before winter, and the squirrel's storage of nuts, we are increasingly involved in putting food away—saving some of this season's abundance for the winter months ahead. Broccoli, tomatoes and pesto have been stored in the freezer. Grapes, rose hips and crabapples are being turned into jams and wine, and cucumbers will be pickled. The garlic, shallots and onions are stored in mesh bags, and the peppers have another month to ripen before they are hung up to dry.

Hatched last April, Suzanne's Barred Rock hens have just started to lay their tiny pullet eggs, and the baby ducks are growing as fast as the tomatoes ripen, getting noticeably bigger each day.

This is my favorite season for flowers: the asters and goldenrods in such long-lasting abundance, the slowly deepening pink masses of *Sedum* 'Autumn Joy,' the wonderful blues of the butterfly bushes and the *Caryopteris*. The annu-

154

als, deep pink zinnias and large flowered marigolds have achieved a wonderful fullness. The orange marigolds are especially exciting interplanted with the parsley in front of the blue-green broccoli plants. The flowers are the site of intense nectar-gathering activities by a marvelous diversity of insects, including the honeybees who are busy putting away food to raise their young next spring.

The most thrilling insects this past week were the Monarch butterflies who appeared, a dozen at a time, on the golden honey plants, the *Tithonia,* and the dark dusty pink *Eupatorium maculatum,* also called Joe-Pye weed. They sucked the nectar to fuel their journey to Central America. What a way to travel.

They also remind us of the connections between our backyards and the rest of the world. These butterflies, like the songbirds, require a healthy and diverse environment in many places to complete their life cycle. The cutting of forests in New England and Central America, and the mowing, paving and sodding of our fields all lessen the survival possibilities of many of the wonderful creatures with whom we share this planet. If each of us takes care of our backyard in a way which protects diversity and native species, and we allow the native people in other parts of the world to do the same (free from the military, financial and corporate pressures of central control), we have a chance of continuing to see the butterflies and birds which so brighten our days.

Scale and Distance
September 18 & 19, 1992

A writer from Indianapolis called several days ago. He was finishing an article for *New Scientist* magazine on evolving methods of pest control which use genetic engineering. He wanted an organic perspective. His call brought into focus the importance of scale and distance.

For years I've been one of the many people working to steer the agricultural establishment toward organic agriculture. We've done this because it didn't make sense to treat our food with toxic chemicals—substances which have been around for only the last few decades of our millions of years of co-evolution with our environment. Aside from this direct effect, however, the chemical approach has produced hazardous wastes, groundwater pollution, and toxic workplaces for manufacturing and farm employees.

Another problem with conventional agriculture is its reliance on energy-intensive chemical fertilizers which can kill soil life, pollute the water with nitrates, and pollute the air by releasing gases which increase the greenhouse effect. Furthermore, these pesticides and synthetic fertilizers disrupt and discourage the use of natural processes and cycles which have aided farmers for thousands of years.

There are other serious effects too. Food production has become concentrated on fewer, larger farms. The distance between the farm and the consumer—that is between the green plants and our mouths—has greatly increased, and there has also been a dramatic increase in the size, importance, control and arrogance of the few large corporations which dominate that space between the farm and our table. As that distance grows, so does the percentage of our food dollar claimed by the corporations in the middle. Energy-use and waste-production also rise.

In answering the questions of the writer from Indianapolis, it became clear that although the agricultural establishment is turning away from toxic chemicals (by manipulating plant genes to get them to produce their own insect or fungus repellents in this case), the most serious effects of the current system may not be eliminated by a shift to organic. We need to grow organically, for sure, but small scale and local are also important issues. The agricultural and food establishment hasn't begun to question scale and distance issues, probably because it is both the cause of, and the beneficiary of this distant, large-scale approach.

Researchers are still asking, "How do we grow more food?" Government and corporate success in answering that question has made overproduction a major problem in American agriculture. Overproduction drives down the price farmers get for their crops and increases the profitability of the gigantic food traders and processors. Frequently, as farm prices go down, consumer prices go up.

Among my more reasoned answers were several more radical statements: that the blame for many of the numerous problems in the cities can be laid to policies which have driven smaller farmers and native people all over the world off the land and into cities with chemicals, giant machines and plentiful cheap food. This has been of greatest benefit to the giant multinational food, grain, beverage and fast-food corporations whose profits increase as farmers receive lower prices and consumers become a captive market, paying higher prices and eating more highly-processed foods. The food industry turns out 16,000 new products each year.

I also told the writer that among the most important agriculture I knew was the 1,000-square-foot garden at Hallen School in Bridgeport, created from an asphalt playground 18 months ago. I was thinking of the previous Friday, our first workday in the garden this year, and of the energy and joy of the 30 fifth-graders. They dug up half a bushel of beautiful potatoes and cut down dozens of sunflowers, their heads up to 2-feet across and loaded with seeds, one of the children's favorite foods. The students also planted lettuce, radishes and spinach for fall harvest, and they weeded wildly. Over the next several weeks, that harvest will provide math lessons, essay topics and food for these students, with an excitement and context which boosts the quality of learning. Of course the school garden is organic. A large, distant farm, no matter how organic, can't provide food of that quality and experiences with that much relevance.

Multinational food giants want to achieve, in the words of one of them "world dominance in food." And we thought the former Soviet Union had a mission!

Only such useful, pleasant and radical actions as creating school, home and community gardens, and actively supporting local farmers, can keep our food from being dominated by a few enormous corporations.

Iced Tea
September 17 & 18, 1993

I've hit upon a nice mixture of herbs for a delicious and satisfying cold tea. I pick 2 or 3 kinds of mint, some bee and lemon balms, and red clover flowers. In a gallon of water, I use about a dozen 8-inch stems of the herbs and maybe a half cup of the flowers. The herbs and flowers are stirred into boiling water which is then turned off. The tea gives off an elegant fragrance. It is good to drink as soon as it is cool enough, but will develop more flavor if it stands overnight, before being strained into jars for storage in the refrigerator. The taste varies with each batch, but we like to have the peppermint and spearmint flavors stand out.

I thought of this tea last Friday at the school compost system in Bridgeport. Several of the fifth-graders were preparing to turn the partially decomposed materials into an adjacent bin and harvest the finished compost underneath for digging into garden beds before planting fall greens. First we had to remove the non-biodegradable trash which accumulates everywhere these days. It's my habit to look at the corporate logos on the little chip bags and beverage containers to see who's successfully marketing their products to these urban children. I was shocked to find the logos of 3 large corporations on an empty iced tea can. (This can brought to mind the old joke about how many bureaucrats it takes to screw in a light bulb. Even as a teenager in Virginia I could make iced tea. Now it takes 3 global corporations?)

This iced tea in an aluminum can was produced by a joint venture of Nestlé, the world's third largest food company, from Switzerland, and Coca-Cola, the world's largest soft drink company, based in Atlanta. Together their revenues last year amounted to more than $1 billion a week, every week, and their liquid assets total over $4 billion. This iced tea was first sold in the Republic of Korea in 1991. Last year it was introduced into the United States, Italy and Taiwan. The same flavor all over the global marketplace. The cans are already showing up in our compost piles.

This can was made by America's third largest can maker, The Ball Company, one of the 14 billion aluminum cans it shipped last year. There were over *92 billion* aluminum cans produced in America in 1992, one a day for each person in the country. Sixty percent of these were recycled at a cost of between $250 million and $500 million. Thirty-six billion cans were thrown away.

These 3 large companies, and others like them, are committed to continued rapid growth, especially by encouraging the people in Asia, Africa and Latin America to drink their beverages out of aluminum cans. Every time we buy these beverages, we cast a vote of approval for this growth, and we also provide the money for it. The largest food and beverage companies in the world are building new factories and buying smaller companies all over the globe. There's no shortage of funds for this growth.

159

Yet, back in the schoolyard, we find out that there are 35 children in each second grade class, and 32 in a fourth grade class. In each class, just one teacher for more than 30 young students, with not enough desks or books. The school system administration's main concern is bringing up the standardized test scores.

The building and grounds people are more worried about removing grass from the playground's sand than glass from the asphalt which covers most of the schoolyard. They plan to add another coat of asphalt this year.

Be that as it may, the new principal, a woman from the neighborhood, is having a very positive effect, and many of the children are excited by their Hallen School Community Garden. This fall the students will make iced tea from herbs they've harvested and store it in reusable containers.

It will be another step in the process of redirecting resources from creating wants in distant places to satisfying needs in our communities.

F A L L

S U M M E R

S P R I N G

W I N T E R

Year 2, Number 1
September 20 & 21, 1991

One year ago, I began these *Living on the Earth* broadcasts. They were dedicated to the proposition that we need to evolve a new relationship with our planet. Understanding the flows and cycles of the natural world, we should use direct, energy-efficient and environmentally-sound approaches to obtain our basic needs. These approaches will include wider solar energy-use and a greater reliance on the bounty of green plants. Individual actions, education and community alliances are needed to work toward a future which we can look forward to and live with, all over the Earth.

This past year has seen an oil war, terrible storms, volcanic eruptions, and the dissolution of the Soviet Union. It has also seen the world's population increase by over 90 million people, in spite of the deaths of over 14 million children under 5 years of age. Twenty-six billion tons of topsoil have been lost and we Americans have used up one quarter of the 23 billion barrels of oil which the world consumed last year. The number of refugees, homeless, and unemployed keeps rising. The coming winter looks bleak for many people who won't have enough food to eat.

The operating principle of our current business and political leaders suggests that we can live our lives disconnected from the environment, enclosed in cars, offices, houses, malls, theme parks and resorts. Energy and food are treated as commodities which can be shipped wherever in the world people can either pay the most for them, or capture our attention with their desperation.

We are denied direct knowledge of how our life style affects others. If our sugar comes cleanly wrapped in neat little packages from the store, for example, we do not connect it with the terrible exploitation of workers and the land on sugar plantations in the tropics. Mass culture and bureaucra-

163

cies obscure our awareness and connect us instead to brand or team names and artificially-defined nations.

And yet, as Wendell Berry says in the preface to his book, *Home Economics*, ". . . the understanding of connections seems to me an indispensable part of humanity's self defense." Until we understand the effects of our lives on the environment and its inhabitants, we cannot begin to improve things.

Pulitzer Prize-winning poet, Gary Snyder, a long-time advocate for native people and their traditional life styles, is joined by the most recent issue of *Time* magazine in calling attention to the importance of the knowledge possessed by these people who still live lives closely connected to their environment. For them, food and energy are the substance and the product of their life style. Their needs are met by the resources of their place on Earth. From that interaction with plants, animals, weather, water and people, their culture has developed.

Without that local connection and direct knowledge of the environment, it is impossible to live in harmony with the Earth. Many civilizations, including the Mesopotamians, the Persians and the Romans have found out that without a sustainable relationship to the environment, civilization disappears.

Because the native peoples of the world have learned how to keep their civilizations going for thousands of years, they are the real success stories of how to live on the Earth. That we continue to destroy their civilizations in our relentless search for cheap oil, beef or electricity is an indication of our serious disconnection.

Economics, which doesn't include social, environmental, government regulatory, or resource-depletion costs in the equation, is a major culprit in bringing us to the point where almost no region or country is self-sufficient.

As we work toward the future, we need to be aware of the importance of scale in our activities. We should realize that more local and bioregional organization and control are needed for sustainable and effective use of plants and the sun. And, we are challenged and stimulated by the increasing diversity of the ethnic and racial mix of an ever-growing population.

Autumn begins at the equinox next Monday. The lowering angle of the sun and cooler nights as well as all the sights, sounds and smells, tell us about this season and our place in it.

Fall 1992

September 25 & 26, 1992

We've just passed the Autumnal Equinox. The days are rapidly getting shorter as the journey around our orbit takes the sun below the equator.

Queen Anne's Lace, asters, and the goldenrods bloom profusely in all the sunny unkempt places, joined in beauty by early-coloring sumac and dogwoods. The land is full of the ripening fragrances of wild grapes and apples. Tomato and winter squash vines sprawl across garden paths and we feel the tension between the warm days which bring further ripening and the approaching frost which will kill the tender plants, but will also bring extra flavor to Brussels sprouts, parsnips and kale.

The pace quickens as we respond to the need to provision ourselves for winter. We've been gathering herbs and nuts and processing food for storage—salsa, raspberry jam, tomatoes and pickles most recently—capturing the abundance of summer for winter's eating. In summer, it is easy to live in the present, but when fall comes, we begin to think about the future, saving seeds from the nicest plum tomatoes and the earliest ripening jalapeño and cayenne peppers, and selecting the best of the garlic to plant about a month from now.

As we prepare for the future on our planet, like the careful gardener, we should all consider what is best and most valuable, and take care to preserve it. We also want to understand what we do that doesn't work and change our ways.

Almost daily, the signs suggest that our present life styles are past sustainability—that we are going down a dead-end road—that the biological and physical processes of the Earth are being stretched to the breaking point. Fierce hurricanes in Florida and Hawaii, record floods in Iowa and Pakistan, persistent droughts in California and Africa—all these may be a preview of the changes we've wrought in the climate. But one thing is clear: It is not the Earth that will break, but our life styles. Left to itself, the natural processes of south Florida will regrow an ecosystem, the sea and the weather will continue, but our lives are severely disrupted.

Not only our environment, but also our society, is suffering. Riots in Los Angeles, a doubling in the number of homeless families seeking shelter in New York City, and volatility in global financial markets are all as likely results of our current relationship with the Earth as are air pollution and the increase in cancer rates and immune system damage.

Recently, President Bush said in Detroit that he wanted our economy to nearly double in size (to $10 trillion) by the early years of the next century. In Colville, Washington, he called "faith in technology" a virtue that will allow us to protect both jobs and nature. Both of these approaches have gotten us into trouble before. Together, they are a recipe for disaster. The same crowd that brought us nuclear power, Agent Orange, Love Canal, DES, Thalidomide and Bophal, now want to bring us genetically-engineered foods, personal communicators and a global financial system. If our faith in technology hasn't been shaken yet, we're not paying attention.

The Earth cannot tolerate a continuation in the growth of our society, or a continuation of technology's attack on the health of the planet and its inhabitants.

Fortunately, there is another road to take—the road to a sustainable future. This is a future with growth in wisdom and happiness rather than in barrels of oil consumed. In this future there will be an increase in the quality of all lives, not an increase in the gross domestic product. A growth in conservation strategies for energy and materials will simultaneously save us money and limit the damage our lives inflict on the Earth. This road leads to a greater reliance on solar energy, the bounty of green plants, and the holistic efficiency of diverse ecosystems.

This is the beginning of the third year of *Living on the Earth*. Besides sharing the joys of gardening and the wonder of the Earth, another goal has been to guide us to that future which will simultaneously improve our environment and the quality of our lives, increase equity and justice everywhere in the world, and preserve democracy. These strategies will also bring each of us in closer touch with the natural world which so shaped and enriched the lives of our ancestors.

Melinda's Garden
September 27 & 28, 1991

Melinda called to find out what book I would recommend to a beginning gardener who wants to produce more food next year. She's grown a few vegetables along her fence for several years, and is a serious composter. Now she wants to start a new plot next spring by rototilling some of her lawn.

"Wait," I said, "if you want to grow vegetables next year, you should start your garden this fall. And, although I think we ought to use the number of acres of lawn turned into gardens each year—the LTG, or Lawns-To-Gardens Index—as a measure of the health and sanity of our society, rototilling in the spring won't work very well."

Of course her garden will be organic; she's feeding her family. The most important aspect of garden preparation is building fertile soil in order to provide the conditions needed to grow healthy plants. The soil ecosystem improves with care and time, so that working this fall to prepare your garden, and planting a cover crop for the winter, will produce a much better soil than you could get by starting next spring. Also, you'll be ready to plant those vegetables which do very well if sown early in March.

The first step to establish a garden is to take a soil sample and get it tested. Then you know what you are starting with. (Most Land-Grant colleges offer soil testing for a small fee. In Connecticut, the Agricultural Experiment Station in New Haven offers free soil tests. In any case, ask for organic recommendations.) Beware of putting your garden in a picture-perfect, weed-free lawn. It may have residues of herbicides or other chemicals which will require special treatment.

Forget the rototiller. For a garden the size a beginner should consider, it's like using a chainsaw to sharpen a pencil. The rototiller also just chops up the grass roots, and many of them will grow again, interfering with your vegetables. I think it is best to lift the sods, in 6 inch by 1 foot sections and compost them near the garden until the grass is killed.

With the grass out of the way, it is easy to turn the soil with a shovel and take note of its color and texture. The darker it is and the more the soil has an irregular crumb structure, the better it is to start with. The presence of earthworms is a very good sign. Loosening the soil down a foot or two will make it easier for your vegetables to grow. Don't worry much about rocks. Remove the large ones, but don't be compulsive about the small ones which get in the way only for root crops (like carrots).

168

Wait for the results of the soil test before you add limestone or other minerals, but every soil benefits from the addition of some good compost or well-rotted manure. It is almost impossible to put too much of these in your garden. With the soil test results you will probably add some limestone as a source of calcium and magnesium and to raise the pH, rock phosphate for phosphorus, and wood ashes or greensand for potassium.

In October, you should plant a cover crop. This is a covering of plants which protects the soil, looks beautiful in the winter, and adds nutrients to the garden next spring when you turn it in. I have used winter rye alone in the past, but this year will try mixing in some hairy vetch. Vetch is a legume which grows well with the rye and provides nitrogen.

And once this is done, the garden cares for itself through the winter, and will be ready, after turning in the cover crop, for planting next spring.

Melinda had wisely chosen a part of her yard which gets full-day sunlight, won't be shaded by trees for years to come, and is not wet or poorly drained. Other considerations are the relationship of the garden to the kitchen, water supply, tool shed and compost area.

I later learned that the book which I had recommended is out of print, but there are others which are also helpful.

Kill Your Television

October 1 & 2, 1992

For several years a radio essay has been lurking around my computer, waiting to be written. Named after a bumper sticker that always makes me smile, it's called "Kill Your Television." Suzanne objects to that title because she feels it is too violent. But here goes, anyway.

The catalyst for this writing is a fascinating new book called *The Age of Missing Information* by Bill McKibben. In it he compares the information he got by watching all of one day's programming on a 93-channel cable system, with the information he experienced during a 24-hour camping trip in the Adirondack Mountains. It brought a lot of things into focus.

Since 1977, Jerry Mander's book, *Four Arguments for the Elimination of Television*, has impressed me. His first argument is that TV confines, narrows, and controls what we are capable of experiencing and knowing. Most of our senses are *not* engaged by television. Smell, touch, taste, and peripheral vision begin to atrophy as sight and sound command our attention. The second argument posits that it was inevitable that TV would be used as an instrument of "psychic colonization" and human domination. Our neuro-physiological responses to electrons beamed into our eyes, which may include physical damage as well as suppression of conscious thinking and creative imagination comprise his third argument. The fourth is that the very nature of television means that it hardens the edges of any information that it presents, creating narrow minds receptive to the simplification of consumer culture. The technology itself is *not* neutral.

Wendell Berry has some wonderful thoughts about TV in his book, *The Gift of Good Land*. In the essay "Family Work," he suggests that you get rid of your television set. "As soon as we see that the TV cord is a vacuum line, pumping life and meaning out of the household, we can unplug it." In

170

the essay, "The Reactor and the Garden," he praises positive actions such as gardening over negative ones like protesting a nuclear plant. His notion of an ideal negative action is to get rid of your TV set, not by selling it or giving it away, but ". . . by disassembling it with a heavy blunt instrument. Would you try to get rid of any other brain disease by selling it or giving it away?"

More recently in *Sports Illustrated* and *Business Week*, I've seen articles about television's future written with the wide-eyed wonder of a 10-year-old boy. The human male sits in an easy chair with a remote control, commanding a giant screen that accesses 500 channels and has the ability to switch or mix them at the touch of a control. The sports buff can create his own instant replays or watch several games simultaneously. Surround-sound, TV shopping and other wonders abound.

But no matter how big the screen, or how many channels there are, TV remains a two-dimensional electronic image with sound that puts somebody else's program into your head. And the bottom line of any TV program is to make us want something we didn't want before. As the chief executive of the world's largest ketchup maker said, "Once television is there, people of whatever shade, culture, or origin want roughly the same things." If what they wanted were peace, education, community, it might be okay. But, as Wendell Berry says, television provides "the overwhelming insinuation that all worth experiencing is somewhere else and that all worth having must be bought."

Almost every program on the tube is there because it is successful at getting people to watch commercials. The average American child will see between 350,000 and 640,000 commercials by the time she reaches 18. The national average of 30 hours of viewing per week was borne out recently by an informal survey of fifth-graders in Bridgeport. That's 5-10 hours per week of commercials alone.

This is the reason why many of us who carry out real processes such as gardening, measuring, or cooking with

171

school children, are so opposed to the trend toward more TV in schools. One of the main problems in education is that our children watch too much TV already. And they have too few direct, real experiences. They have seen everything on TV and think they know and can do everything. Like TV itself, this is a dysfunctional illusion.

Our appreciation of the richness and pleasure of life without TV keeps growing. Try it yourself.

What's a Recovery (from Recession)?
October 4 & 5, 1991

Economists, politicians, and business people are all looking for "the recovery" and checking the vital signs— unemployment, orders for durable goods, sales of cars and homes, consumer confidence, and growth of the gross national product—hoping to announce that the recovery has begun.

What's a recovery? In the way it is frequently used, as in "He's a recovered alcoholic," it means giving up some addiction to return to a more balanced state. The current recession is a direct result of our economy's addiction to greed and the energy-intensive approach of the last decades. It's also a result of our simple-minded use of money as the determinant of our actions.

The message of the media, however, is that we want to get those numbers up there again for the recovery—build and sell more cars, construct more high-rise office towers, manufacture and sell more plastic things. The shorter the life of the products we buy, the better. That means we'll need more garbage trucks and incinerators, and can go back to the store for even more plastic stuff. There are still a few miles of

172

road which aren't completely lined with strip malls and some acres of farmland which haven't been converted to overpriced subdivisions filled with houses that don't even know where the sun rises.

With all this, of course, we'll need more roads, more completely refurbished gas stations selling snack and junk foods, and more parking garages. We'll have to build more airplanes to accommodate all the business travelers and, while we're at it, build a few more nuclear power plants, drill for more oil to power all the new cars and energy-intensive buildings, and select more sites to deal with our increasing household, radioactive, hazardous and toxic wastes.

Should we be concerned that this kind of recovery creates places everywhere which are inhospitable? The major highways which literally bulldoze through and over almost every town create zones of noise and pollution. Energy and waste facilities create areas that are off-limits to humans, and subdivisions are almost as empty in the daytime as downtown office zones are at night.

In the early part of this century, a major automobile manufacturer, a tire company and an oil company got together with a vision. They bought Los Angeles's efficient mass transit system and dismantled it. It's not clear whether they were greedy, stupid, or just believed in a future where all of us sit in ever more expensive cars on bigger and better superhighways.

We Americans are now less than 5 percent of the world's population, yet we own over one third of all the cars on Earth. We consume (by burning or turning into plastics or chemicals) over one quarter of the oil that is used in the world. From the burning of fossil fuels, the United States emits 50 percent more carbon dioxide per capita than the former Soviet Union, almost twice as much as West Germany, more than twice as much as Japan, and almost 9 times as much as China. If the Earth has environmental problems now, think what it will be like if the rest of the

173

world follows us down the dead-end road of high energy consumption, and catches up.

We need a recovery, all right. The recovery we need is to rediscover our relationship to our planet—to develop nurturing instead of exploitative relationships with the Earth and the plants, animals and humans with whom we share it.

Like any sick person in the process of recovery, an addict is helped by good nourishing food, clean air and water, quiet, rest, and the love and care of family and friends. When he or she is able, interesting, useful and meaningful work helps to build a good self-image and satisfaction.

The vision of those who helped put the automobile at the center of the American economic religion has turned into the nightmare of clogged roads, urban slums, decayed mass transit systems, runaway factories, polluted air, and food that travels more than 1,300 miles before we eat it.

Let's actively work toward a vision of the future which includes more trees and gardens, clean air and water, less waste, and satisfying, ecologically-productive work everywhere.

Now that's a recovery.

Harvest
October 9 & 10, 1992

The harvest and cold weather keep us hopping these days. Last week we fought off the frost in our pepper patches with old bedsheets and tarps, hoping for more ripening when it got warm again. Some of the varieties we didn't cover were barely bothered, especially the ancho, jalapeño and Argentine purple peppers. In any case, when we pull the plants and hang them up, the fruit survives and will continue to ripen and turn red even if the plants have been injured by the frost.

Tomato, cucumber and squash vines which used to sprawl everywhere, suddenly disappear with the first frost, but the fruit usually is not harmed, though it needs to be harvested before the next frost.

The sweet potatoes were injured first, over 2 weeks ago. They are very sensitive and need to be dug soon after frost turns the leaves black. Of the 3 varieties we grew, 'Centennial' was the most prolific, 'Jewel' produced nicely and 'Puerto Rico' didn't do well, in part because of the cold summer.

One of the real success stories each fall is the Butternut squash harvest. This year, 3 seeds planted in one hill and ignored until harvest produced over a bushel of fruit. There are other squashes we like the flavor of better than Butternut—Buttercup and Delicata, for example. But over the years, Butternut has demonstrated a wonderful sturdiness. It resists vine borers and squash bugs, and usually produces lots of those beautiful orange-fleshed tan squash which store so well.

We left most of the potatoes in the ground until last week. Besides harvesting the blue potatoes (whose skins have the deep complicated coloration of old fountain pen ink), we harvested Yukon Golds and several hills of "volunteers" which grew from the compost piles. That night Suzanne turned some of the gold potatoes into pancakes, shredding them with onion and garlic, and adding a little flour and a couple of fresh eggs. They were fried in a small amount of oil. Hold the sour cream: We made fresh applesauce from the fruit of wild apple and crabapple trees with a little local honey and a touch of nutmeg. How delicious *and* healthy too, because those apple trees have never been sprayed. The fruit's not so great to look at, but it makes a wonderful sauce.

After gardening for years, we realize that in the natural world a blemish-free fruit is the exception. Sure, a good gardener can grow some. But between insects and birds, diseases, weather and mechanical damage, frequently the fruits and vegetables that are available in the garden have holes or other imperfections. When we cook using fresh produce from the garden, we see how little these flaws matter. The first step in the kitchen, after washing if needed, is usually cutting, and if we have to cut out a spot, or bruise, it's no big deal—just food for the compost pile or chickens.

I thought I'd write something about next Monday's anniversary of Columbus's arrival, but I got caught up in the excitement of the harvest and good food. Then I realized that tomatoes and their relatives the peppers, yellow, white, and blue potatoes, the unrelated sweet potatoes (which are cousins to morning glories), beans and winter squash are all plants which originated in what's now the Americas. We should add corn and sunflowers, among others, to this list. They are all native to the so-called "New World" and, through thousands of years of careful selection and cultivation here, have evolved into important foodstuffs.

These plants in our gardens connect us with over 7,000 years of successful life in this land before the Europeans arrived to find what many of them described as a paradise. Like native food, we find that the culture and traditions of the original Americans have much to teach us.

About a year ago I came across a quote from Kirkpatrick Sale that I thought was very interesting, if somewhat hyperbolic. In *The Conquest of Paradise: Christopher Columbus and the Columbian Legacy*, he concludes, "There is only one way to live in America, and there can be only one way, and that is as Americans—the original Americans—for that is what the earth of America demands. We have tried for five centuries to resist that simple truth. We resist it further only at the risk of the imperilment—worse, the likely destruction of the earth."

I've thought about this ever since. It seems less hyperbolic all the time.

May you enjoy a bountiful harvest.

The Human Diet

October 16 & 17, 1992

The hydrogenation of edible oils to make margarine was one of the first applications to our food supply of an industrial, rather than a biological process. It was developed in France in 1869 as a response to industry's appetite for edible fats and oils in the days before petroleum. This process uses nickel as a catalyst and hydrogen under high pressure and temperature to convert liquid oil into semi-solid fat.

It has been discovered that margarine, especially if made with large quantities of artificial fats (hydrogenated vegetable oils) may be harmful to our cholesterol levels and hence to our hearts. Hydrogenated fats and the trans-fatty acids seem to be the real culprits, and are found in more than just margarine today. They are also used in crackers, pastries, cakes, doughnuts, French fries, potato chips, puddings, imitation cheeses, frozen fish sticks, ready-made frostings, candies and chicken nuggets. Note that most of these foods either didn't exist until recently, or were relatively rare in our ancestors' diets. They are also manufactured in places that look much more like factories than like kitchens or gardens.

News reports feature anxiety-ridden consumers who don't know what to believe about food and how to eat. However, if we study our history, this new information shouldn't be surprising.

Since we emerged as a species between 200,000 and 500,000 years ago, human biology has been relatively unchanged. Our bodies extract energy and nutrients from food in the same way as the bodies of our distant ancestors did. Until 10,000 years ago, we got all our food by hunting animals and gathering plants and their fruits, seeds and roots near our homes.

About that time some of our ancestors began to cultivate grains for food, and they started to control animals in a way that led to their domestication. Hunting and gathering persisted. This means that for at least 200,000 years our diets changed little from generation to generation, altered only by the slow but effective evolution of food plants through selection and cultivation, and by the effects of migration, increasing knowledge of food plants or early trade. Ancient ways persist to this day as we gather berries or mushrooms, catch trout, hunt deer or quail and tend our gardens.

Until the last few generations the human diet had certain broad and continuing characteristics: Our food came from our immediate environment and varied with the seasons. Animal fats were probably rare, available only after the exertion of the hunt, or the hard work of farming. Food preservation was accomplished by simple, effective, home processes like drying, fermenting, smoking or salting. An indication of the effectiveness of these processes is the fact that cheeses, yogurt, authentic soy sauce, sauerkraut, some sausages and wine are all produced by various biological fermentation processes. And most of us humans were directly involved in obtaining and processing our food. This not only allowed us to spend a lot of time outdoors using our bodies, it also provided each of us with important knowledge of the plants and animals in our environment and of the practical science of food processing.

Margarine was just the beginning of our food supply's industrialization. In the last few decades, industrial agriculture and the global food and beverage giants have nearly taken over our eating habits. We spend our lives entirely inside and our food travels thousands of miles. Thanks to global food marketeers, people all over the world can eat the same food, year-round. Industrially created artificial colors, flavors and preservatives are added and mixed in such varieties that the food industry can turn out 16,000 new products a year. Irradiated and genetically-engineered foods, synthetic fats and sweeteners and packaging innovations are the new industrial ingredients of our diet. And much of what is done to our food (from the toxic fungicide mixtures sprayed on fruit to keep it from rotting on its 3,000 mile journey—to

178

the bacterial genes spliced into tomatoes, potatoes and soy-beans to make them resistant to herbicides) is done for the benefit of other industrial processes, not for our good health.

Fortunately, there is another growing trend. From the famous chefs who reject genetically-engineered foods—to nutritionists who recommend more whole grains, legumes, fresh fruits and vegetables—to the swelling ranks of home and community vegetable gardeners and local organic farmers, there is a vision of a future food supply more in keeping with our history. This should also reduce health-care costs, cut energy-use and waste production, and give us gardens instead of food factories.

Nuts

October 18 & 19, 1991

Leaves aren't the only gift we receive from the trees this time of year.

Delicious and nutritious chestnuts, hickory nuts and black walnuts are lying on the ground, waiting to be gathered and eaten or stored.

I noticed that the large shagbark hickory in the fence row had nuts on the end of almost every branch which had become visible after most of the leaves had fallen. After finding my way through the brush to the area under the tree, I discovered hundreds of nuts that had already dropped. The thick green husks of many of them had split open, each depositing a one-inch-diameter nut on the ground.

Other hickories produce nuts too. The pecan is a southern hickory. The bitternut, mockernut and pignut hickories produce nuts which are bitter or very hard to shell. Shagbark nuts, on the other hand, are large, with a wonderful flavor, and are relatively easy to shell. Hickory trees can live for hundreds of years and grow to over 100-feet tall. The wood from these trees, very strong and resilient, was used by the Wright Brothers for their plane and is still used for tool handles.

American chestnuts were the most important deciduous trees in the forests of the eastern United States until the early years of this century. These tall, magnificent trees produced more than a prolific crop of nuts; their wood was beautifully colored, light and easy to work, yet durable enough to be used for fence posts, split rails, and animal stalls. Some old houses have interior walls made of chestnut boards which are as wide as 2-feet.

Chestnut blight, a tiny disease organism introduced from the Orient just before the turn of the century, wiped out most of the chestnuts in just 2 decades.

Chestnuts sprout from the roots after the top is killed, so there are still some of these trees around and progress is being made on a biological control for the blight which may someday restore the chestnut to our forests. In the meantime, Chinese chestnuts and their hybrids with the American chestnut are resistant to the blight, and are therefore a good choice. I planted a half dozen or so over 15 years ago. They are now producing a bumper crop of nuts.

The nuts from the Chinese trees are larger than the American nuts, but the trees are lower and more spreading, so they don't produce such fine lumber.

The black walnuts I planted are still young and haven't produced much this year, but I've been harvesting these highly flavored nuts from a parking lot in New Haven. The natural packaging of walnuts is so sturdy that the cars only manage to remove the outer husk. The nuts, still in their shells, can then be gathered. Like the American chestnut, the black walnut produces very valuable lumber. With a beautiful dark color, good working characteristics, and strength, it is a fine wood for furniture and paneling.

Of course the reason these trees produce nuts is to reproduce themselves. In the wild, or in our yards, squirrels may eat many of the nuts, but the chances are that they will bury some for storage and forget about a few. If conditions are otherwise appropriate, a new tree will grow. The incredible profusion of these nuts reflects the small percentage which will find suitable conditions for germination and growth.

Hickory and walnut trees are in the same family. They have taproots which make them difficult to transplant once they are more than a few feet tall, so planting nuts is a good way to begin.

Many of us are familiar with Rainforest Crunch, made with cashews and Brazil nuts. One of the purposes of this candy is to provide a market for the products of a living rain forest in order to help preserve it. From a global perspective, it is shortsighted to buy this candy while we allow our own forests to be cut down and ground up by giant chippers to make way for shopping centers, pipelines, subdivisions and highway interchanges.

The tropical rain forests and our temperate forests are both endangered by the misguided notions of progress and economics. All of the Earth's forests will be helped by our greater appreciation and sustainable use of these resources.

In Making Compost
October 20, 1990

In making compost, what we are doing is nourishing life. Living things need access to water, air, and food and to get rid of their wastes. If we provide the right conditions, the beneficial composting bacteria and fungi will do the work.

Composting is the aerobic process whereby plant wastes are converted to stable humus compounds which are very beneficial in the soil for growing trees, shrubs, vegetables,

181

flowers and lawns. There are many different ways to compost. With the proper balance of air and water, a compost system will be nearly odor-free.

The topsoil in New England was built up by the slow, steady composting process which takes place in the debris layer on the forest floor. Except for lawn areas, it is probably good to allow leaves to stay on the ground under trees and shrubs, to insulate and protect roots and soil life through the winter and to slowly release nutrients.

For a large quantity of leaves we need to create a system that works more quickly than the forest floor. A greater mass (a cube, 3 feet or more on a side), more frequent turning, and smaller pieces will speed up the process.

When materials are composted, their volume is greatly reduced. Carbon dioxide and water are returned to the air as the elaborate solar energy-collecting structures of the plants (their leaves) are broken down and converted into other substances.

The materials in the compost should have the dampness of a wrung-out sponge. Too much water will exclude air, causing an anaerobic fermentation which emits a bad odor. The solution is to turn the pile in order to incorporate more air. It is useful to mix in a little good garden soil to provide some of the necessary composting organisms.

The food needs of the composting organisms can be compared to our dietary requirements. Evidence suggests that we should eat plenty of complex carbohydrates for energy and a smaller quantity of animal protein for cell building and repair. The compost organisms need a lot of carbonaceous materials (such as brown leaves, sawdust or straw) for energy, and a smaller quantity of materials high in nitrogen (such as green grass, weeds, manures or kitchen wastes) to build proteins.

Your compost system can be as simple as a pile or as fancy as a wire or wood container or purchased bin.

Fill it with leaves this fall and add food wastes through the winter. With each addition you can stir the compost and check on its progress.

In making compost, we are not just helping to solve the solid-waste problem. We begin to change our thinking from the linear-mechanical model, which has gotten us into so much trouble, to the cyclic-biological model which brings us in closer harmony with our planet.

Leaves
October 23 & 24, 1992

One morning after a humid and warmish night, as the early rays of the sun hit the persimmon tree, its leaves fell off in a steady flow.

The ash trees dropped their yellow leaves last week, letting welcome fall sunshine into places which had enjoyed their shade only weeks before. About the same time, the white pines dropped the needles they didn't need any more, creating a beautiful covering on everything underneath.

Leaves from the sugar maples fell in yellow and red splendor before those from the swamp maples. The hickories lost half their leaves some time ago, and now hold on to the rest; the beeches will retain many of theirs much of the winter.

Black oaks, their leaves ranging from yellowish brown to deep maroon, all with the depth and sheen of well-worn and cared-for leather, let their leaves go slowly. Eighty years of attentive living in this area have convinced my friend Sam that the way the leaves hang on the oaks (i.e., in the top, bottom or middle) foretells the amount and timing of snow for the coming winter. The rarer white oaks, more evenly scarlet, hold their color longer.

Each of the wild dogwoods seems to have a different

coloration and rate of change. The kousa dogwoods also have a variable coloration several weeks later. The weeping willow (one of the earliest trees to color in the spring) the magnolias and the filberts are still green.

For weeks the leaf color display has been as impressive on the paths as in the garden and on the distant hills. The pleasant crunch and color of the leaves underfoot is one of the special joys of this season.

With creative planting, you can have a long period of beautiful colors in a small area. Besides the dogwoods, sweetgum, *Stewartia* and *Oxydendrum* trees all have wonderful fall leaves. Doublefile and maple leaf viburnams, blueberries, oak leaf hydrangeas, many deciduous azaleas, some ferns, poison ivy and Virginia creeper have especially beautiful coloring.

Notice the difference between the area under a tree in the woods, and the ground under a tree whose leaves have been raked year after year, causing the soil to become thin and packed with more roots exposed.

We will be well on our way to ecological sanity if we can all understand that the leaves that fall this time of year are a special and valuable resource. They provide insulation and food for the soil and its inhabitants during the winter, and for the plants that will grow there in the coming years. Leaves contain stored solar energy and minerals mined from underground by trees, which while living, provide air conditioning, oxygen, clean air, food, and beauty, and at the end of their lives, fuel and building materials for people or the decomposers.

Instead of being used as a resource, leaves are often viewed as a nuisance to be cleaned up, and as an opportunity to sell resource-depleting plastic bags and the leaf blowers which so pollute the stillness.

Leaves can be left everywhere they fall except on lawns, paved walks, gutters and wooden structures. A few leaves won't hurt a lawn. More leaves can be dealt with by chopping them with a mower to add organic matter to the soil. A thick covering of leaves may harm the grass and can be removed. The fact that it is really beneficial to let the leaves stay under trees and shrubs suggests that with less lawn, we can rake less. One of the ways to convert from a lawn to a garden is to cover the lawn with between 6 and 12 inches of leaves.

Leaves that are raked up should be composted nearby for eventual return to the soil. Anything from a simple pile at the edge of the woods to an elaborate compost system will allow leaves to turn into good humus.

GATT and Democracy
October 25 & 26, 1991

As we are distracted by the scandals, greed, and petty partisan bickering in our nation's capitol, larger and more far-reaching issues like the General Agreement on Tariffs and Trade (GATT) are being pushed to completion by the Bush administration.

I have read about concerns regarding the effect of GATT on farms in publications from organic farmers in New England and family farmers in the Midwest. I know that farmers in France and Japan are against some of GATT's provisions. It wasn't, however, until the recent straightforward reporting in the venerable British publication *The Economist*, that I really understood GATT's implications. When and if we sign this agreement, it will supersede our laws in a way that actually jeopardizes our democracy.

The specific issue here is tuna imports from Mexico versus the American people's desire to protect dolphins—those intelligent and playful marine mammals. In the eastern

185

Pacific Ocean, dolphin and yellowfin tuna swim together, the dolphin near the surface and the tuna below. Tuna fishing with purseseine nets can result in the death of many dolphins. Our representatives in Congress passed the Marine Mammal Protection Act which prevents American fishing fleets from using methods that endanger the dolphins. The 1990 version of the law prohibits the import of tuna caught by methods that kill 25 percent more dolphins than the limits imposed on the American fishing fleet. Mexican fishermen don't meet this stipulation; they may be killing 50,000 to 100,000 dolphins per year. Under U.S. law, passed by our representatives in Congress and interpreted by our courts, imports of Mexican tuna were banned.

The Mexican government challenged our action before a GATT panel in Geneva. The panel's ruling said, "A contracting party may not restrict imports of a product merely because it originates in a country with environmental policies different from its own." This ruling not only says that we can't restrict imports of the tuna, but it also has implications for elephant tusks, foods grown with pesticides that are illegal in our country and even the arrangements made for controlling ozone-destroying chemicals. To the extent that we abide by GATT, this 3-man panel in Geneva has overruled our elected officials. Yes, 3 men, completely removed from our electoral process, have that much power.

We should understand clearly that President Bush is one of the world's greatest backers of GATT and other free trade arrangements. *The Economist* reports that it was a Bush administration suggestion which encouraged Mexico to appeal to the GATT Panel.

Thankfully, GATT isn't fully worked out yet. European farmers have managed to delay it. They wisely believe that farms and local food production are more important than the abstract notion of free global trade.

Look at what free trade does. It puts everywhere in the world in competition with everywhere else. Whichever country has the most attractive mix of low-paid labor, lax environmental and chemical regulations, and tax benefits for business, will attract global corporations until another country offers better tax benefits. Farms in Europe, Japan and the United States which have produced food for hundreds of years will be driven out of existence by global businesses that take advantage of poor countries and cheap energy to produce food far from its eaters.

The big winners in the GATT Agreement (and its strong backers) are global corporations, especially energy, transportation, chemical and consumer products companies and the world's monster-sized banks.

There are many voices among our people saying that GATT will result in further environmental damage, loss of jobs near home, and the loss everywhere of the security that local self-reliance provides. This would be bad enough. The abstract notions and the realities of free trade and global competition are not worth the loss of our voice in government—not worth the loss of democracy.

History for the Election
October 30 & 31, 1992

Last week I was speaking to the Ridgefield Earth Alliance, which, like groups in many towns, brings concerned and committed citizens together to share information and consider solutions to local and global problems.

This talk took me back 12 years to the end of the 1970s when I was also speaking to groups like this. It was near the end of Jimmy Carter's presidency. Our dependence on foreign oil *and* our export of weapons had again gotten us into trouble in the Middle East. This time Americans were being held hostage at the American Embassy in Tehran.

Back then, there was a plan to move away from those expensive and connected addictions. I was one of hundreds of State University Cooperative Extension Service personnel around the country who were providing education and advice to encourage energy conservation and renewable energy-use. Admittedly, all was not rosy. Although many of us were interested in the passive-solar, greenhouse and garden-with-shade-trees approach to renewable energy-use, the oil companies wanted to sell solar panels filled with toxic fluids—but that's another story. In any case, we energy agents helped millions of families, communities, schools, businesses and government units to conserve energy. Conservation is a very powerful strategy which lowers costs almost everywhere it is applied, while it reduces the need for and pollution from fossil fuels and nuclear power plants.

Then the conservatives won the 1980 election and tossed conservation out the window. They had a $3 trillion debt to run up and couldn't have government officials driving around in energy-efficient cars. Solar water-heating panels were removed from the White House, and the Environmental Protection Agency's car fleet average dropped to 6 miles per gallon.

For years the new administration bought as many energy-intensive weapons systems as would seem possible. Many of these, like the shiny office palaces sitting empty which enriched developers and S&L directors (and cost us $500 billion in S&L bailout money), are now useless and expensive either to maintain or to take apart. Like nuclear power plants, they will continue to demand energy and resources for a long time into the future. Is it in spite of, or because of our high-tech weapons that we do such a poor job of keeping the peace in our cities, and educating, housing, and nurturing our children?

We can supposedly deliver a smart bomb down a chimney with ease, but we aren't very good at delivering food to starving people.

Twelve years ago, in the last year of Carter's presidency,

the United States Department of Agriculture published the "Report and Recommendations on Organic Agriculture." This document said that organic farming addresses and solves some of the most serious environmental problems of agriculture, while it also provides a good financial return to farmers with many sizes and types of operations.

President Reagan made sure that the author of that report was fired, and that his work was shelved and ignored. As a result of that policy, millions of tons of unnecessary, harmful fertilizers and pesticides and their manufacturing wastes were dumped on United States' soil.

Nevertheless, the inescapable trend away from these expensive and polluting energy-intensive inputs continues, as threats to our water supply make local organic agriculture even more attractive. Small organic farms and gardens are proliferating from within our inner cities to the distant hills.

Solar photovoltaic cells now power emergency aid call boxes and light billboards along our highways, and utility companies provide subsidies for energy-saving light bulbs because that is the cheapest way to get new power. The elegance and wisdom of conserving not just energy and resources, but also species, cultures and ancient knowledge are becoming ever more obvious.

Twelve years later, south-facing windows, shade trees and gardens still work very well. I know that I can safely recommend them to my great-grandchildren, just as my great-great grandparents might have to me, had I known them.

For the solar and conservation direction he encouraged, as well as for his continuing work for peace, fair elections and affordable housing, President Carter deserves our respect and thanks.

When we vote November 3, we need to pay attention to history and have a clear idea of the challenges ahead. It's going to be a long process. But, as the trees and vines which are reclaiming our crumbling inner cities demonstrate, green plants and the sun will eventually prevail. The sooner we realize this, the more likely it is that humans will be around to enjoy a bright and green future.

Potato Chips and the Transfer of Wealth
November 6 & 7, 1992

Here's a quote from the *1991 Annual Report* from PepsiCo, one of the world's largest snack food companies. "During the next decade, the core group of snackers—the 10 to 20-year-olds—is projected to grow twice as fast as the overall population. We are introducing products and package sizes especially for this new generation of snackers." They cite a new cheese flavored snack in the shape of a cat's paw. "The unique shape captured the eyes and taste buds of children and retail sales of this new product exceeded $80 million in its first year."

Recently, I pulled an empty, flavored potato-chip bag out of the trash in Suzanne's fifth-grade classroom in Bridgeport. Here's a math problem for the kids. If 2 ounces of chips cost 75¢, how much do these chips cost per pound? Potatoes are frequently advertised at $1 for 10 pounds or 10¢ per pound. It took the students a while to convert to pounds and figure out the cost of the chips, but we got to the answer—$6 a pound.

The kids did the math, but I saw another problem. What's really going on here? We have a very cheap raw material, potatoes, which becomes very expensive after processing and the addition of frying and flavoring ingredients. This represents a markup of 5,900 percent! These fifth graders know how easy it is to grow potatoes. They harvested a good crop from their schoolyard garden which had been asphalt just 2 years before.

We tried to think about what this phenomenal markup paid for. The kids suggested transportation, the oil for frying, the other ingredients, profit, advertising, workers, plants and equipment, and packaging. It still seemed excessive, especially considering that as the maker of half of the snack chips in this country, PepsiCo probably buys its potatoes at considerably less than local retail price, say at a few cents a pound. These chips are fried in whichever mix of the 9 oils listed is cheapest and most available, and then coated with salt and 11 other ingredients in lesser quantities, including 3 different milk products and by-products, chemicals, more sodium, and artificial color. PepsiCo's *Annual Report* says, "The overall cost per pound of materials used to produce our products has not increased in the last 10 years." It seems likely that, since the second-largest ingredient is oil, and this bag contained about a tablespoon, the food ingredients for this 75¢ bag cost less than 5¢. And, most of these ingredients are very inexpensive because of government and environmental subsidies to the energy, corporate farm, and agrochemical industries.

I was also astounded that these children, who have lots of unmet needs in their lives, many of whom get free lunches, who attend a school without a full-time nurse, without enough books or chairs—these same children are able to send such profits to a global concern. PepsiCo, which also sells soft drinks and operates 29,000 fast-food restaurants worldwide, boasts that it has doubled its sales and net income every 5 years for 26 years. Its CEO says it is his company's intention to keep up this growth rate, doubling every 5 years, *forever.*

The chips in question contain twice the recommended percentage of fat in our diets and nearly a whole day's supply of sodium. Although potatoes are one of nature's most wholesome foods, and one of the few foods we could live on exclusively, when peeled, fried, salted and coated with chemicals, they become a prime example of what many nutritionists say is unhealthy about American diets.

The teacher says that the kids become very restless and irritable about a half hour after they eat their chips at snack time; they crave water and want more chips. Imagine what even a few kids behaving that way among 30 in one room can do to the educational process.

Of course, these children's parents and guardians, whose high local taxes don't fulfill their children's educational needs, pay increasing amounts for the disposal of all the packaging that PepsiCo can sell with its chips.

Over the last 10 years, directly and through our taxes, our costs for education, health care, energy subsidies, oil wars and waste disposal have risen dramatically, while this global food corporation quadrupled its sales and profits.

Before we make snack foods as available to everyone in the world as they are to Bridgeport's children, we should examine the connection between our increased costs and the swelling profits of this and other global corporations.

Disingenuous
November 8 & 9, 1991

Webster's Seventh New Collegiate Dictionary defines the adjective disingenuous as "lacking in candor, giving a false appearance of simple frankness, or CALCULATING."

Disingenuous is not a word I use frequently, but it jumps out as the perfect word to describe a recent 9-page full color special advertising section in *Time* magazine called "America's Favorite Places."

The cover page of this special section sponsored by Jeep Eagle, the 4-wheel drive vehicle maker, invites us to explore our nation's breathtaking beauty with 4 champions of the environment, 3 entertainers and a wilderness ranger.

Then, right up front, the ad gives a strong clue to its rationale. The automobile-maker's poll found that Americans said the environment is one of the most important topics of our time. So it isn't hard to see why they now use the environment to sell automobiles.

Across the bottom half of each 2-page spread is a photograph of a beautiful canyon, beach, mountain, or sunset, each with a different model automobile, looking as if it had been dropped into the real scene by helicopter or into the photograph by a computer.

The texts, one by each of these champions of the environment, reinforce the sense of the pictures in the ad, of the special wonderfulness of wild places, and of the joys of relative solitude in those places. One 4-wheel-drive vehicle will get you to these places. More vehicles will likely ruin the solitude, and perhaps the wilderness with their noise and pollution. Praising unpolluted solitude and selling cars to get there is almost perfectly oxymoronic, isn't it?

This contradiction alone seems bad enough, but the disingenuousness goes further. To almost everyone whose livelihood doesn't depend on cars and their fueling, it is clear that the Earth would benefit from fewer gasoline powered automobiles. Our cities and highways are clogged, parking lots are full, and our air is polluted. More land is now devoted to cars than to housing. That yellowish haze streaming off the eastern end of Long Island isn't just from factories and jet planes. Our government is in deeper financial trouble because of taxpayer subsidies to the giant energy producers and the automobile's infrastructure.

Given the short attention spans of many of us, the images of the vehicle and a beautiful environment together may have more impact than the prose, which is a shame. Singer/songwriter John Denver reminds us that "any place that brings us in touch with nature is special and to be cherished." He includes such places as neighborhood parks and backyards. He also says, in talking about finding a balance between people and nature, "In Alaska, we see the need to conserve and protect our greatest natural treasures—even to the extent that we may have to sacrifice some of the technology the human mind has given us." Actor Lou Gossett, Jr. reminds us that the great natural treasures weren't always far away. He remembers as a child, catching crabs for his family and neighbors near the docks in Brooklyn. He recalls, "It was reassuring to have the Atlantic Ocean nearby as a reliable source of food for the family when times got tough."

The 165 million cars in America consume 12.2 million barrels of oil per day, and hundreds of billions of dollars in indirect costs per year, leaving behind dirty air, parking lots, gas stations and highways which make huge areas inhospitable to other life forms. Our society's emphasis on automobiles rather than mass transit makes second-class citizens of those who are either too poor or too advanced to purchase a car. Because of our role as a world leader, and because there will be over 3 billion cars on Earth if everyone has as many as we Americans have, we should lead the way in designing a future with less dependence on automobiles.

Automobile ads showing beautiful environments are disingenuous in the same way as cigarette ads which feature healthy, active, beautiful young people. Perhaps like cigarette ads, they should carry a warning label: The use of automobiles causes smog, resource-depletion and urban decay.

The Solar-Powered Clothes Dryer
November 10, 1990

The Solar-Powered Clothes Dryer is the last of the *Big-Four, Low-Cost, Ready-to-Use Solar Collectors Designed for a Better Tomorrow.*

I've talked about the organic vegetable garden as the most important solar collector. On the equinox, I mentioned the combination of south-facing glass for warmth and well-placed trees for cooling as two more sensible solar technologies. The clothesline completes the quartet of energy savers everyone with a backyard can use.

Since people started wearing clothes, they have dried them in the sun or around the home fires. The well-planned landscape design early in this century included a drying yard. Only in the last few decades have people grown accustomed to using fossil-fuel or electric energy to provide drying services. Nostalgia for the fragrance of sun-dried clothes is so strong that the markets are full of chemical products that make machine-dried clothes smell, well... sort of like sun-dried ones.

The clothesline is a good example of the benefits and responsibilities associated with low-tech solar solutions. They are inexpensive, with low (or no) annual maintenance or energy costs. Unlike the electric or fossil-fuel solution, the negative effects aren't somewhere else. These technologies require individual action and connect people more directly to the environment upon which we depend.

Some may say that hanging clothes on a line is inconvenient. Compared to the inconvenience of storing radioactive waste from electricity-generation for 100,000 years, or with the inconvenience of a 1-to-3-foot rise in sea level, stronger hurricanes and a loss of the Great Plains as fertile farmland because of the greenhouse effect, hanging clothes to dry is very convenient.

Some may say that clothes hanging on a line are ugly. We have to compare that ugliness to a stripmine, an oil spill or a gas pipeline in our back yard.

You might ask, if clotheslines are so wonderful, why aren't they promoted? The answer is that our government likes to provide us with energy by giving tax breaks and subsidies to large corporations so they can produce energy to sell to us. When we buy that energy, the government taxes us to pay for these subsidies to the corporations which sell us energy. It has been recently estimated that government benefits to, and environmental subsidies and health costs of the fossil-fuel and nuclear industry, amount to over $1,000 per year for each man, woman, and child in our country. That's a total of over $250 billion per year.

Some apartment dwellers may not be able to hang their clothes on a line. This is an indication of one way that our society has evolved in response to cheap subsidized energy. Our homes, food, work and play demand a large quantity of energy because government subsidies have encouraged energy-use. Our national debt, balance of trade, deteriorating environment, and clogged roads are all a direct result of government and industrial energy policies. We can search for military and technological solutions which will encourage us to keep using enormous quantities of energy. Or, we can design a future that takes maximum advantage of the sun shining on the whole Earth every day.

The Hidden Costs of Energy
November 13 & 14, 1992

As a nation we will not make much progress on our government's fiscal problems, or in cleaning up our environment, until we bring the hidden costs of our oil and nuclear energy addictions into our daily consumer decisions.

In April 1991, *Scientific American* used a cartoon to illustrate its article titled "The Real Cost of Energy." This cartoon shows an American motorist in her car at a gas station with a soldier pumping gas. The station's sign lists regular gas at $1,001.29, and unleaded at $1,001.39. While pumping gas, the soldier explains that, "this gas is only $1.39, the aircraft carrier is $470, the tank is $125, the Stealth fighter is $330, the gas mask is $45 and the gun adds $30 a gallon."

Although the numbers are a little high, it makes the point very well. The article notes that in 1989 alone the Department of Defense spent between $15 billion and $54 billion to safeguard oil supplies in the Persian Gulf. Taken with the $30 billion the Persian Gulf War was estimated to cost, the lower of these hidden defense expenses equals

$23.50 for each barrel of imported oil. A week ago, Saudi Arabian light crude cost just $16.95 per barrel.

Besides military costs, the *Scientific American* article lists direct subsidies, employment and crop losses, corrosion, health impacts, and radioactive waste as other categories of our energy system's hidden costs. These hidden costs are paid for with our taxes, directly out of our pockets, or both. One of the simplest of these expenses to quantify is the direct government subsidies through tax credits and research funding. This amounts to $50 billion per year, or about $200 from each person in this country. (By the way, every time you hear that the government is going to spend a billion dollars, remember that is about $4 from every person in the United States.) Of this $50 billion subsidy, about half goes to fossil fuels which supply about 85 percent of our energy. Nuclear power gets 40 percent of the subsidies, even though it now provides less energy than renewable sources which get only 10 percent of the subsidies.

There are some disagreements in total costs for health effects, radioactive waste and crop losses, but all told, the authors estimate that we pay between $100 billion and $300 billion each year in hidden costs for our energy. This produces higher taxes, reduced services and a lowered quality of life equal to between $400 and $1,200 per person, per year. This affects everyone. The urban apartment dweller who walks to work bears the same proportion of this hidden cost as the suburban commuter with 3 cars, 2 houses and a heavy airplane-travel habit.

If gasoline were twice as expensive, we could move closer to our work, buy a more efficient car, car pool, walk or take public transportation to reduce our costs. With the current system, we can do all those things, and we *still* pay the hidden costs. If we paid twice as much for heating oil, we would be encouraged to conserve energy (by insulating, caulking and weather stripping our homes) and to use solar energy.

Just a note about energy figures. The above estimates don't include long-term costs like acid precipitation and global climate change. The government figures for total energy use do *not* include the solar energy collected by south-facing windows, and the human energy used for transportation or gardening, for example. And there are indications that the $400 to $1,200 per person, per year, figure mentioned above may be low. World Resources Institute just published *The Going Rate: What it Really Costs to Drive.* The authors of this report found that even excluding vehicle cost, fuel, insurance, and repairs, automobiles directly cost over $600 per person, and indirectly cost between $2,000 and $3,100 per person, per year in the United States, even if you don't own a car.

These hidden costs distort the energy market, encourage profligate energy-use and discourage conservation.

They will keep rising until we pay them directly when we fill up our cars, throw a pair of socks in the dryer, or buy a single-use, throwaway container.

Adaptation
November 15 & 16, 1991

L
ast April, the National Academy of Science's panel on global warming issued its report which said that atmospheric concentrations of carbon dioxide and methane (both of which trap heat) had risen significantly in the last century and were continuing to rise, primarily as a result of human activities. Global average temperature has also risen during this 100-year period.

This report suggests modest steps for reducing our emissions of these heat-trapping gases, including increasing the efficiency of our buildings, automobiles and transportation system, all of which would save more money than they cost.

198

When you insulate your house, both your fuel bill and your greenhouse-gas emissions are reduced for the life of the house.

In September, after a summer that included record strings of above 90 degree days in the Northeast, a second panel from the Academy, this one on adaptation, issued its report. This panel assumed that global average temperature and sea level will rise. "What will be the impact?" it asked. "Can we adapt to it?" Over the objections of several members, the panel concluded that our speed of innovation and the turnover rate of capital investments are both faster than the projected rate of climate change. The only exceptions are natural ecosystems which have slower response times and therefore are harder to "climate-proof."

The panel concluded, with some caveats, that we shouldn't take drastic measures to protect ourselves. Instead, we should concentrate on steps which deal with current climate fluctuations—steps like building insulation, disaster management, controlling development of low coastal areas, and diversifying water supplies.

There are a number of threads to weave together as we try to make predictions about our climate in the future. One of the most complicating factors is the Earth's dynamic weather. Our spinning globe, orbiting the sun to produce the seasons, includes oceans which act as heat-storage mechanisms and give birth to cyclones and hurricanes which are heat-transfer mechanisms. The day-to-day and year-to-year variability of this complex system makes it hard to say that any given weather event is anomalous or inconsistent.

Another thread includes our continuing discoveries about the atmosphere and the Earth. Chlorofluorocarbons (which destroy the ozone layer) were thought in the April report to be a greenhouse gas, but have since been discovered to have little net effect on global warming. This means that the cutbacks in their use, which we will make to protect our grandchildren's skin, won't help us with the greenhouse effect.

199

The inertia of human behavior and of our economic system, with its reliance on massive fossil-fuel and nuclear-energy flows, tends to keep us going in the same direction—toward less self-reliance anywhere, and greater dependence on large entities and distant sources everywhere.

The final thread is the way we try to predict the future. The adaptation panel relies primarily for its upbeat report on what atmospheric scientist Stephen Schneider calls "a surprise-free scenario of mild, predictable change." As reported in the magazine *Science*, it was only after Dr. Schneider objected to this scenario that the panel added some caveats warning that catastrophic effects are possible, and if this is the case, adaptation will be neither cheap nor easy.

About a month after this Adaptation Report was released, 3 major disasters occurred at about the same time on the 5 percent of the Earth's surface which our country occupies. What appeared in the hills as just strong winds was an unusual storm from the north Atlantic which caused record high tides, large waves and a great deal of damage along the east coast. In the upper Midwest, record amounts of snow fell in an early storm. Meanwhile, on the west coast, 4 years of drought and human settlement patterns set the stage for especially strong winds to turn a small fire into a major inferno.

All of these disasters could be 100 percent natural. Or they could have been caused or made worse by human activities, the way clear-cutting of hillside forests in the Philippines made the recent cyclone-carried rains there so much more deadly. We just don't know.

What we do know is that local, diverse, small-scale systems are likely to be more stable and less prone to catastrophic failure than large, centralized ones.

Abundance: Thanksgiving, 1991
November 22 & 23, 1991

On Thanksgiving, we traditionally express gratitude for the blessings in our lives with a meal that recalls the Native Americans' sharing of New England's abundance with the English newcomers.

When the Europeans arrived here almost 400 years ago, they came upon a people who had lived in the area for 10,000 years, a people who had evolved a complex and sophisticated relationship with their environment. The way the Indians managed and lived in the ecosystem resulted in incredible abundance. Yale University historian William Cronon provides tantalizing glimpses of New England at the time of its colonization in his thought-provoking book, *Changes in the Land: Indians, Colonists and the Ecology of New England.*

He quotes many writers from the 17th century who were astounded by the bounty of food, fiber and wood in New England: enormous herds of deer and elk, banks of oysters, flocks of turkeys, quail and grouse, schools of fish, profusions of berries, nuts, fruits, and herbs, each for the taking in its season. The Natives made much use of fire and selective clearing to create conditions suitable for wild and cultivated food plants and the animals which used them. Cronon writes that when the Indians hunted game animals, "In an important sense, they were harvesting a foodstuff which they had consciously been instrumental in creating . . . For New England Indians, ecological diversity (whether natural or artificial) meant abundance, stability, and a regular supply of the things that kept them alive."

Cronon makes it clear, however, that most of the newcomers had no idea that this abundance wasn't a gift from God or an ecological accident. The English failed to realize that the abundance they experienced was the result of active ecosystem management which had made life successful there

201

for 10,000 years.

Let's compare this native abundance with a more modern example of abundance. Fifteen years ago, I visited a wheat farm in North Dakota. The farmer grew a square mile of wheat using all the energy-intensive machinery, fertilizers and pesticides of modern agriculture. His storage bins were full of wheat and he had more in the fields. Surplus production pushed the price down below 8¢ a pound, less than it cost him to produce it. As I arrived, his wife was unloading groceries from her car, groceries which included fluffy white bread and processed, boxed, ready-to-eat wheat cereal. Each of these food items consisted mostly of wheat similar to that which he couldn't sell for 8¢ a pound, but which cost over $1 a pound in its processed and packaged form.

Although I had seen national overproduction drive successively larger dairy and egg farmers out of business in my own town, analogous to the way overproduction has driven airlines, banks and contractors out of business, I was amazed when I read a history of the United States Department of Agriculture. As far back as the 1930s, overproduction of food and fiber was a serious problem which was putting farmers out of business. In fact since then, only World War II and its aftermath were able to soak up the overproduction of American farmers.

And yet our tax-funded public, and tax-deductible corporate agricultural-research establishments continue to try to answer the question of how to increase production. From the early days of fancier machines, to the latest genetically-engineered growth hormone for cows, the research has almost exclusively produced products for the industrial economy to sell to farmers, products which simultaneously encourage ever larger-scale farm production facilities and ever greater dependence by the farmer on outside inputs. Many of these products have also greatly increased the energy-use and environmental damage done by farms and by our food system.

We need to ask different questions and solve other problems with our agriculture.

If we ask how to get the freshest, most delicious and nutritious food in a very resource-efficient and ecological manner, we get an answer that includes organic gardens almost everywhere.

If we ask how to use agriculture to lower health-care costs and improve education, the answer includes a garden at every school.

This Thanksgiving, Suzanne and I are thankful for our garden which is still producing food, and for the fifth-graders at Hallen School in Bridgeport who love to learn in their garden and eat the food that they grow.

The Soil
November 24, 1990

As we remember fondly the Thanksgiving feast just past, let's consider the real source of that food—the soil.

Except for seafood and hydroponically-grown vegetables, there would be no food without soil. Yet we call soil dirt and, through intention and neglect, it has become one of the most besieged parts of our environment.

The soil is a complex ecosystem which is alive, taking in oxygen and giving off carbon dioxide, digesting organic matter and supporting a vast and incredible quantity of living organisms.

A single teaspoon of fertile soil contains over 6 billion living things. (At one a second, it would take you almost 200 years to count the living organisms in that single teaspoonful of soil!) A physician friend once said he could sterilize surgical instruments in good garden soil because it contains such a variety of benign organisms that pathological organisms can't survive. Researchers have recently found that well-made compost has this kind of effect on soil-borne disease organisms that attack potted plants. In an artificial environment, the benign organisms in the compost simply outgrow the pathological ones.

Soil is made of 4 parts—mineral, organic, air and water. The mineral portion consists of ground rocks of various sizes, ranging from larger particles (which are sand), through mid-size particles (silt), to clay, which has very small particles. The organic portion of the soil consists of living things—fungi, bacteria, algae, nematodes, protozoa and worms—as well as the remains of these living things and the plants which grow in and above the soil. The living organisms are constantly breaking down mineral particles, organic matter, and the air, and thereby release nutrients which other soil organisms and plants can utilize.

The nature and balance of the mineral and organic portions determine how much air and water are in the soil. Sand easily lets water flow through, and invites air in. Clay holds water and excludes air. Without the proper balance of air and water, living things in the soil can't thrive. Humus (decomposed organic matter) is an almost magic ingredient which helps sandy soils hold water and brings air into clay soils. The complex structure of humus provides an enormous surface area to hold nutrients and environments which are hospitable to microorganisms.

The soil, which is biological, suffers from being treated with the products of our industrial-mechanical thinking. Our soil is under attack from chemical fertilizers which burn up the organic matter. Insecticides, herbicides, and fungicides injure soil life and upset its balance. This chemical attack has spread from American farms to our lawns, and to places around the world.

Industrial farming practices in the Midwest are causing soil to be washed away by erosion faster now than in the dust-bowl years. Acid precipitation releases toxic elements in the soil, and composted sewage sludge spreads toxic heavy metals over what are called "non-food producing" areas.

Much of the organic matter—leaves, yard and food wastes—which, if composted, could help build and hold soil, is still being taken to the landfill or incinerator. Overgrazing and excessive cutting of trees injure the soil in many parts of the world. And in Connecticut we practice the ultimate insult—covering the soil with asphalt.

As the population of the Earth increases, we need to remember the importance of soil. No civilization has ever outlived its fertile topsoil.

Free Goods
December 3 & 4, 1992

The World Health Organization estimates that 1.5 million babies die each year from "bottle baby disease." That means 3 babies die every minute because they miss the protection from disease and malnutrition that exclusive breast feeding for the first 6 months of life provides. Breast feeding also often acts as a natural contraceptive which lowers fertility rates, and it improves the health of mothers and infants.

In economic terms, breast milk is a free good. Seven thousand generations of mothers have made use of this free good to nourish their babies and establish an important bond with their children. Whether we believe that the Earth's inhabitants were created by a wise supreme being, or are the result of the marvelous, 4-billion-year evolution of life on a well-situated planet, the idea of a female mammal providing exclusive nutrition to her young in its early life has real elegance and wholesomeness. Mother's milk is the reason for breasts.

But breast milk is useless to a corporation's bottom line.

(It should be noted, in contrast, that breasts themselves are frequently very useful, especially to entertainment and publishing corporations. For this use, however, a baby would just get in the way.)

Breast milk doesn't make the gross domestic product swell. It makes breasts swell with its natural blend of perfectly-balanced nutrition and disease-fighting antibodies. Breast milk has the advantage of being uncontaminated—a real bonus in the many parts of the world where the water isn't fit to drink. That water, used to mix formula, can cause the cycle of diarrhea, dehydration and malnutrition called "bottle baby disease."

If a company wants to sell breast milk substitutes, it needs to persuade women to turn their backs on a free good and buy infant formula. Here, the formula makers can exploit a fact of nature. If a woman's milk isn't used, it dries up and can't be restarted. In that way, infant formula is like cigarettes. Try it for a while and then you're hooked. Giving out free samples is a good way to get steady customers.

Pictures of healthy babies on free cans of formula in clinics all over the developing world encourage women not to breast feed, even though as UNICEF's executive director has said, "In the developing world, the decision not to breast feed increases the risk of death 10 to 15 times in the first 3 to 4 months of life." Even in some developed countries, bottle-fed babies have a higher incidence of disease.

Eleven years ago, in response to free supplies and deceptive marketing practices in the Third World, the World Health Assembly adopted the *International Code of Marketing of Breast-milk Substitutes.* It took 3 years and a consumer boycott to get some global corporations to agree to abide by the code. Since then, the International Baby Food Action Network (which represents 148 groups in 74 countries working for better infant health) has monitored compliance. Their publication, *Breaking the Rules,* details hundreds of examples of deceptive marketing practices in 80 countries. These reports have prompted organizations from 14 nations to participate in a new boycott of the worst offenders—Nestlé and American Home Products. These organizations include the very conservative Church of England, Presbyterian women in this country, middle school students in West Haven and college students at SUNY Brockport, to name a few.

This issue powerfully demonstrates one of our economic system's most serious problems. Because it doesn't value free goods, it encourages predatory behavior against them. This results in large profits for the predators at great cost to individuals, communities and societies everywhere.

For more information, contact Action for Corporate Accountability, 129 Church Street, New Haven, CT 06510, (203) 787-0061.

Economics
December 6 & 7, 1991

It is not so much that we have an economic problem. It's more like economics *is* the problem—economics and our myopic attention to it.

Let's consider what economics is and is not. It is not a set of natural laws, like physics or chemistry. It is a human construct, more like the rules created for a card game.

Economist Hazel Henderson thinks that economics is the malfunctioning strand in the DNA code of our culture, and that it will keep replicating its pathology until it is corrected. She believes that one of the problems with economics is that it makes unreal assumptions. These assumptions and the boundaries that economics creates, assign great value to some things and no value to others; this produces far-reaching social changes.

A glance at a typical college economics text from the 1960s shows how this happens. After saying that the field of economics studies how human wants can be satisfied as much as possible, and identifying commodities and services as the goods which satisfy human wants, the author then carves out a big exception: the non-economic wants.

The book explains that non-economic wants are satisfied by goods that do not exist or by goods that are free. Pay attention to what the author leaves out of the realm of economics. His first category of non-economic wants includes wisdom, courage, love, peace, justice, and freedom. Since there are no goods which can satisfy these wants, they are outside the realm of economics.

The second category of non-economic wants is satisfied by goods that are free. The only example given in the text is air. I might have included sunlight, rainfall, and perhaps the fantastic number of plants, animals, and smaller life—the incredible diversity—that is found nearly everywhere on Earth. Non-economic goods could also include such things as stillness and traditional culture, for example.

In the broadest sense, we could say that the Earth itself is a non-economic good. If we assume that non-economic goods are free and inexhaustible, they become devalued and vulnerable. The assumption that air is free has encouraged the large-scale manufacture of automobiles—machines that suck up clean air and spit out dirty air. But what may seem free for a single car on a country road is certainly not so free near a clogged highway.

Environmental problems ranging from the loss of diversity to most kinds of pollution result from the inability of economics to really value this Earth that we inhabit. By putting love and courage, striving for peace and freedom outside the economic system, economics devalues the incredible energy that these nearly universal human tendencies generate. The love and protection that a mother gives her child is powerful and pervasive. It is enhanced by breast feeding. But breast feeding is outside the realm of economics. Except for the too-numerous malnourished mothers of the world, breast milk is a free good.

Economics solves the breast feeding problem with infant formula, an economic good which uses more energy, produces more waste, is more expensive and frequently less beneficial to the physical and emotional health of the infant. Yet the central role we have given to economics has produced the situation where the promotion and advertising of infant formula is tax-deductible, and breast feeding is a non-economic activity threatened by the formula-makers.

The world of economics logically produces junk bonds, junk mail and junk food, billboards advertising cigarettes and alcohol, prurience and violence in the movies and on TV, professional sports overload, S&L failures and state-promoted gambling. It produces these undesirable effects because it is not able to value most of the things which make us human: the activities we do for love—the oldest and most important human activities. These include for example, a father's teaching of his children, a daughter's care of her parents, volunteer work in the schools, growing our own food, and reveling in the beauty of the Earth.

We can't fix our problems with economics because it excludes what really matters.

By giving economics the upper hand, we have created an obscene abundance of economic goods and a tragic shortage of non-economic goods.

If we really want peace, justice, wisdom, love and a healthy environment, we need to greatly diminish the role of economics in our lives.

Chickens

December 8, 1990

A small flock of chickens is one of my favorite home food producers.

For ease of keeping, quality of food and fringe benefits (like their manure and the disposal of kitchen and garden wastes), a small flock of chickens is hard to beat. We have just 3 hens. On most days they produce 2 eggs, or just over a dozen a week, about the right number for a small family. These neat packages of high-quality nutrition are always exciting to find in the back corner of the henhouse.

Chickens have a high body temperature and good feather insulation, so given enough ventilation and shade in the summer and an unheated enclosure for the winter, they are easily housed. Of course, in the commercial houses, with 500,000 hens in one building, temperature control gets to be a big problem, but for the home flock of from 2 to a dozen chickens—no problem.

If you allow 4 to 6 square feet of floor area per hen, their living quarters will be in the mansion category compared to commercial hen houses where 2 or 3 hens are stuffed in very small cages. The backyard flock can be let out into the yard often to go on bug patrol. And they are very good at going back into their house as it gets dark in the evening.

Like most other living things, chickens need fresh water and nutritious food. In addition to some grain or laying pellets, they love the overripe or spoiled food from the garden. Many common garden weeds (like chickweed and pigweed) are among their favorite foods. They also need some grit or small stones for their gizzards and ground seashells for calcium to produce the eggshells.

Like us, they need to have their house cleaned a few times a year. This is an opportunity to get a very valuable material to add to your compost pile. If leaves, sawdust or straw have been used on the floor of the chicken house, the manure doesn't smell, and will be on its way to being an ideal fertilizer. When there are half a million hens in one place, the manure is a serious problem. But with a few hens, it becomes a valuable resource.

The henhouse needs to be secure enough to resist the predations of raccoons, weasels and dogs, all of which like to eat chicken.

Hens, like women, produce eggs without the assistance of the male of the species. A rooster, if you want one, will make the eggs fertile, provide some protection for his flock, and function as a fairly reliable alarm clock. The rooster's crow might be the only justification at all for outdated, restrictive zoning laws in many parts of this region which ban the keeping of a small flock of chickens.

The increasing light in the spring will cause the hens to lay more eggs, and as the daylight wanes, egg production slows down. Following the natural cycle, hens can be productive for 2 or 3 years. Commercially, they are stimulated by artificial lights and have a useful life of about one year.

The biggest difference, however, between commercial and home production is the taste of the eggs. Because of the variety of foods that the home flock eats and the freshness of the eggs, they have a wonderful flavor. Comparing commercial eggs and homegrown ones is like comparing a cheap jug wine with a fine vintage. What a difference!

Simply boiled for a packed-to-go lunch treat or turned into an omelet with fresh garden vegetables and a little cheese, you'll love having your own eggs.

Secrets
December 11 & 12, 1992

Why all the secrets? For the third time in about 12 hours, the issue of commercial secrecy has come up as a roadblock to intelligent decision-making and the pursuit of knowledge.

The first secret came in the course of researching a school breakfast. I wondered about the cost of the disposable plastic bowl containing $^{13}/_{16}$ (or just over $^3/_4$) of an ounce of wheat cereal which was the largest item in that breakfast. I calculated that it contained about $^1/_2$¢ worth of wheat, and less than that of vitamin spray. Sugar, salt, malt extract and corn syrup were the only other ingredients. Since they are all cheap and plentiful, and the total weight is less than one ounce, we can safely assume that all the ingredients for the cereal itself cost about 2¢ or 3¢. The manufacturer told me that it couldn't reveal the price the school had paid, but with prompting, the woman on the telephone gave a price of about 45¢. She said that only a distributor could tell me for sure. The distributor called the next day, both defensive and curious, and said that pricing information was confidential.

My current research indicates that a single serving of school breakfast costs taxpayers over $1.

The second secret: The next day, Public Radio's Morning Edition carried a story about the fungicide which has been accused of grotesquely distorting plant growth on hundreds of acres in Florida, and causing health problems for farm workers there. Of course, the manufacturer claims that its product didn't and couldn't cause that damage. Some tests said yes. Some said no. However, the manufacturer (one of the world's largest) wouldn't release the names of the ingredients in the fungicide because they are a trade secret.

Later, as I was doing research for an essay on the James Bay hydroelectric project, the third secret emerged. In this case, it was the rate at which the builder of the gigantic and environmentally- and culturally-destructive James Bay power project was selling electricity to aluminum smelters. To build such an enormous system of dams, roads, power lines, and other expensive accoutrements, the builder needs to have long-term guaranteed sales. The Quebec utility made such agreements with the companies which supply us with electricity and with international corporations which produce aluminum. Although the price paid by the aluminum smelters is a carefully kept secret, estimates are that they pay less than 2¢ per kilowatt hour (kwh), even though the electricity costs 4¢ per kwh to produce, and is sold to customers in Quebec for 5¢ per kwh. It costs about 10¢ per kwh by the time we buy it.

There's a distinct pattern here. The cereal maker, the fungicide maker, and the Quebec utility are all very large corporations which take money out of our communities in exchange for supplying us with food and energy. The Minnesota cereal maker gets our tax dollars for processing and packaging wheat whose growing we've subsidized. The Canadian utility wants our electricity payments to subsidize aluminum makers and ecocide in the far north. The fungicide, even if not as toxic as alleged, creates toxic environments in its manufacture and in its use. The giant dams of the James Bay Project produce nearly genocidal ecosystem disruption and the aluminum smelters create damaging air pollution. Plastic cereal bowls, aluminum foils and cans and agricultural chemicals all end up as waste we must pay for with our money, our health, or both.

The subsidies we contribute to the oil and nuclear industries provide raw materials and processing- and transportation-energy inexpensively enough to make disposable bowls, aluminum snack food bags, widespread fungicide-use and distant-dependency possible and profitable.

These secrets obscure the dangerous insanity of depending on farms a thousand miles south for vegetables, on dams a thousand miles north for energy, and on a giant corporation a thousand miles west to feed our children and ourselves.

213

Bringing in the Greens
December 13 & 14, 1991

As we approach this holiday season and the Winter Solstice—as gifts are frequently and freely exchanged—we should remember one of the greatest gifts we have here on our planet: the Earth's trees.

At this time of year, many of us will bring some greens into our home: holly, hemlock, and cedar boughs, fir, pine and spruce trees. This practice can be traced to the Roman celebration of Saturnalia, and to the Druids' tradition of decorating their huts with evergreen boughs during the winter.

At this time of year, with the sun so low in the sky, and the nights so long, with leaves off the trees, and cold all around, it's not surprising that for centuries people have liked to bring some of these evergreen symbols of continuing life inside their homes.

Saturnalia, the ancient Roman festival of Saturn, was celebrated beginning on December 17; it included the Winter Solstice. The Romans sent boughs and other gifts to friends at this time to honor Saturn, their god of agriculture. To help gather converts, the Christians co-opted this holiday by establishing the celebration of Christmas on December 25, and the giving of gifts. However, an early church edict forbade Christians to decorate their homes with boughs during the pagan celebration.

Meanwhile, in northern Europe, Druids and other pagans are said to have brought evergreen boughs into their huts to provide an abode for the sylvan spirits. Because of their necessarily close relationship with plants, forests and the seasons, these people understood that there are very special aspects of the natural world and the solstice—a turning point in the annual solar cycle.

We may bring in greens because the bright red berries and shiny, pointed leaves of holly are cheering, or because the boughs of fir and ropes of white pine have a delightful

214

aroma. Although we may not be pagans, we are nevertheless carrying on a pagan custom.

In doing so, we should recognize an inescapable fact: Our survival on Earth is profoundly intertwined with the survival of trees. Trees and other green plants are our essential partners here on this planet. Without them, we would run out of oxygen and food. We should remember, however, that trees got along for millions of years without us.

Time and again, throughout history, humans have attacked their forests. The Romans (and especially the central-heating systems in their villas) had voracious appetites for wood. They imported it from over 1,000 miles to the east. As pagan ways faded, overuse severely depleted the forests of northern Europe and the British Isles, also.

Today we are more aware of the many important roles that trees play for us. They clean and cool the air, manage water, and build and hold soil. They also provide food and homes for birds and many other living things. Cities with an abundance of trees are cooler, and houses with evergreen trees to the northwest are easier to heat.

Although they have been under siege before, the Earth's forests have never before been under such a widespread and powerful attack since the last ice age, more than 20,000 years ago. As this destruction of forests spreads, our knowledge of their global importance grows. Destroying rain forests in South America affects the rainfall in Africa. Destruction of forests in the American tropics or in New England, depletes the songbird population which needs forests in both places to survive.

Our trees are under attack, not only from chain saws and bulldozers, but from acid precipitation, excess low-level ozone, depletion of upper-level ozone, changing weather patterns and world-traveling insects and diseases.

So this season, when we bring greens into our homes, let's remember their importance. We are honoring trees for their role in our lives.

215

If you need a cut tree, buy it locally, recycle its boughs as winter covering for your garden, use the chips or heat from the trunk, and plant at least 2 trees next year to take its place. If you plant holly, pine or spruce trees to the northwest of your house, you will have a warmer home and beautiful pruned greens for years to come.

Trees are truly one of our greatest gifts.

Bibliography

Alliance to Save Energy. *America's Energy Choices: Investing in a Strong Economy and a Clean Environment.* Union of Concerned Scientists, 26 Church Street, Cambridge, MA 02138, 1991.

Bell, Michael. *The Face of Connecticut: People, Geology, and the Land.* State Geological and Natural History Survey of Connecticut, 165 Capitol Avenue, Hartford, CT 06106, 1985.

Berry, Wendell. *The Unsettling of America: Culture and Agriculture.* New York: Avon Books, 1977.

The Gift of Good Land: Further Essays Cultural and Agricultural. San Francisco: North Point Press, 1981.

Home Economics. San Francisco: North Point Press, 1987.

Calvin, William H. *The River That Flows Uphill: A Journey from the Big Bang to the Big Brain.* New York: Macmillan, 1986.

Caras, Roger. *The Forest.* Boston: Houghton Mifflin, 1979.

Castleman, Michael. *The Healing Herbs: The Ultimate Guide to the Curative Power of Nature's Medicines.* Emmaus, PA: Rodale Press. 1991.

Coleman, Eliot. *The New Organic Grower.* Chelsea, VT: Chelsea Green, 1989.

Cronon, William. *Changes in the Land: Indians, Colonists, and the Ecology of New England.* New York: Hill and Wang, 1983.

Engeland, Ron L. *Growing Great Garlic.* Filaree Productions, Route 1, Box 162, Okanogan, WA 98840, 1991.

Gershuny, Grace and Joseph Smillie. *The Soul of Soil: A Guide to Ecological Soil Management.* Gaia Services, Box 84, RFD 3, St. Johnsbury, VT 05819, 1986.

Gibbons, Euell. *Stalking the Wild Asparagus.* New York: David McKay Company, 1962.

Gleick, James. *Chaos: Making a New Science.* New York: Viking, 1987.

Gould, Stephen Jay. *Time's Arrow, Time's Cycle.* Cambridge: Harvard University, 1987.

The Panda's Thumb. New York: W.W. Norton & Co., 1980.

219

Grieve, Mrs. M. *A Modern Herbal* (1931). New York: Dover Publications, 1971.

Gussow, Joan Dye. *Chicken Little, Tomato Sauce & Agriculture: who will produce tomorrow's food?* New York: The Bootstrap Press, 1991.

Henderson, Hazel. *Creating Alternative Futures: The End of Economics.* New York: Berkley Publishing Corporation, 1978.

Hubbard, Harold M. "The Real Cost of Energy." *Scientific American*, April, 1991, Vol. 264, No. 4.

International Baby Food Action Network. *Breaking the Rules 1991.* IBFAN/IOCU, P.O. Box 1045, 10830 Penang, Malaysia.

Jackson, Wes. *Altars of Unhewn Stone: Science and the Earth.* San Francisco: North Point Press, 1987.

Jeavons, John. *How to Grow More Vegetables Than You Ever Thought Possible on Less Land Than You Can Imagine.* Berkeley, CA: Ten Speed Press, 1991.

Lappé, Frances Moore and Joseph Collins. *Food First: Beyond the Myth of Scarcity.* New York: Ballantine Books, 1977.

Lovelock, James. *Gaia: A New Look at Life on Earth.* Oxford: Oxford University Press, 1979.
The Ages of Gaia: A Biography of Our Living Earth. New York: W.W. Norton & Co., 1988.

Mander, Jerry. *Four Arguments for the Elimination of Television.* New York: William Morrow & Co., 1978.

McGee, Harold. *On Food and Cooking: The Science and Lore of the Kitchen.* New York: Charles Scribner's Sons, 1984.

McKibben, Bill. *The Age of Missing Information.* New York: Random House, 1992.

New Haven Ecology Project, 51 Perkins Street, New Haven, CT 06513.

NOFA/CT. Northeast Organic Farming Association of Connecticut. Box 386, Northford, CT 06472. Contact for chapters in other Northeastern states.

Olkowski, William and Helga, and Sheila Daar. *Common-Sense Pest Control.* Newtown, CT: Taunton Press, 1991.

PACE. Peoples Action for Clean Energy. 101 Lawton Road, Canton, CT 06019.

Pulsa. "The City as Artwork" in *Arts of the Environment*, ed. by Gyorgy Kepes. New York: George Braziller, 1972.

Reich, Lee. *A Northeast Gardener's Year*. Redding, MA: Addison Wesley Publishing Co., 1992.

Reich, Robert B. *The Resurgent Liberal, and Other Unfashionable Prophecies*. New York: Random House, 1989.

Rodale, J. I. *How to Grow Vegetables and Fruits by the Organic Method*. Emmaus, PA: Rodale Books, 1974. (Out of print, but worth looking for in used book stores).

Rombauer, Irma S. and Marion Rombauer Becker. *The Joy of Cooking* (1931). Indianapolis, New York: Bobbs-Merrill Co., 1975.

Sale, Kirkpatrick. *The Conquest of Paradise: Christopher Columbus and the Columbian Legacy*. New York: Dutton, 1991.

Smith, Marny, and Nancy DuBrule. *A Country Garden for Your Backyard: Projects, Plans and Plantings for a Country Look*. Emmaus, PA: Rodale Press, 1992.

Smith, Miranda, Editor. *The Real Dirt: Farmers Tell About Organic and Low-Input Practices in the Northeast*. Burlington, VT: SARE, 1993.

Snyder, Gary. *The Practice of the Wild*. San Francisco: North Point Press, 1990.

Thomas, Lewis. *The Lives of a Cell: Notes of a Biology Watcher*. New York: Bantam Books, 1975.

United States Department of Agriculture Study Team on Organic Agriculture. *Report and Recommendations on Organic Farming*. Washington: USDA, 1980.

University of California, Berkeley. *The Wellness Encyclopedia*. Boston: Houghton Mifflin Co., 1991.

Watt, Bernice K. and Annabel L. Merrill. *Composition of Foods: raw, processed, prepared*. Washington, D.C.: United States Department of Agriculture, 1963.

Webster. *Webster's Seventh New Collegiate Dictionary*. Springfield, MA: Merriam-Webster, 1967.

221

White, E.B. *Charlotte's Web*. New York: HarperCollins, 1952.

World Resources, 1992–93: A Guide to the Global Environment, World Resources Institute, Oxford: Oxford University Press, 1992.

World Resources Institute, "The Going Rate: What it Really Costs to Drive." WRI, 1709 New York Ave., NW, Washington, D.C. 20006, (202) 638-6300.

World Watch Institute, 1776 Massachusetts Avenue, NW, Washington, D.C. 20036.

Wyman, Donald. *Wyman's Gardening Encyclopedia*. New York: Macmillan Publishing Company, 1977.

Annual Reports

Free by request and packed with information:

Archer Daniels Midland Company, P.O. Box 1470, Decatur, IL 62525, (217) 424-5200.

Ball Corporation, 345 South High Street, P.O. Box 2407, Muncie, Indiana 47307-0407, (317) 747-6100.

Borden, Inc., 277 Park Avenue, New York, NY 10172, (212) 573-4000.

The Coca-Cola Company, P.O. Drawer 1734, Atlanta, GA 30301, (800) 438-2653.

Nestlé S.A., Avenue Nestlé 55, CH-1800 Vevey (Switzerland) or c/o Dewe Rogerson, Inc., 850 Third Avenue, 16th Floor, New York, NY 10022, (212) 688-6840.

PepsiCo, Inc., Purchase, NY 10577, (914) 253-2000.

Philip Morris Companies Inc., 120 Park Avenue, New York, NY 10017, (212) 880-5000.

RJR Nabisco Holdings Corporation, 1301 Avenue of the Americas, New York, NY 10019, (212) 258-5600.